# God in Flesh
## Discovering the Genuineness
## of Christ's Humanity

# God in Flesh
## Discovering the Genuineness
## of Christ's Humanity

# Daniel L. Segraves

# God in Flesh

by Daniel L. Segraves

Copyright © 2001, 2009 by Daniel L. Segraves
Second printing, 2001
Third printing, 2001
Fourth printing, 2004
Fifth printing, revised and expanded, 2009

Printed in the United States by Morris Publishing
3212 East Highway 30
Kearney, NE 68847
1-800-650-7888

"The unassumed is the unhealed."

– Gregory of Nazianzus (330-389)

# Contents

# Preface

This book began as a response to three pages of notes taken by students during my days as a teacher in a Bible college. These students had visited a church where a Bible study was taught claiming that Jesus had "heavenly" flesh and denying any biological connection between the virgin Mary and Jesus. The students took notes during the Bible study and brought them to me for a response.

In 2001 I first published a small book titled *God in Flesh: Was Jesus' Flesh Heavenly or Earthly?* The book went through a total of four printings, three of which were in 2001. The fourth printing was in 2004.

This edition of the book is revised and expanded with the addition of my response to the "heavenly" flesh teaching found in a book titled *Bible Writers' Theology.*[1] There are two chapters in this new edition of the book. The first, consisting of my response to the students' notes, is titled "Did Jesus Have Heavenly Flesh?" The second, my response to *Bible Writers' Theology,* is titled "Heavenly Flesh: A Response."

Daniel L. Segraves

---

[1] Teklemariam Gezahagne, *Bible Writers' Theology* (n.p.: Ozark Mountain Press, 1999).

# Did Jesus Have Heavenly Flesh?

During my days as a Bible college teacher, some of the students visited a church where a Bible study was given claiming that Jesus had "heavenly flesh." These students presented to me three pages of notes taken during the study and wanted my response. The notes consist of a series of Scripture references followed by interpretive statements which, in the final analysis, allege that Jesus Christ did not possess the same human existence that is possessed by all other human beings. This teaching asserts that Mary contributed nothing to the humanity of Jesus. In fact, according to this teaching, Mary was not the mother of Jesus. Somehow, the flesh of Jesus was "heavenly" and "incorruptible." It is further alleged that when believers are born again, they somehow put off the earthy flesh and become partakers of the heavenly, incorruptible flesh of Jesus.

I do not know how accurately the notes were taken during the lecture; I can respond to them only as they came to me. But before the response, I would like to make a general statement about this teaching and offer some biblical insight as to the genuineness and fullness of Jesus' human nature and His complete solidarity with the human race.

## Monophysitism

So far as I can tell, the teaching that Jesus had "heavenly flesh" is a resurrection of the ancient error of Monophysitism. This was the teaching that Jesus had no genuine or meaningful human nature. According to this view, Jesus had only one nature: the divine. His humanity was either different from that of the human race, or it was somehow overwhelmed and consumed by His divine nature.

But the "heavenly flesh" teaching adds to Monophysitism the belief that those who are born again somehow experience a biological change in their bodies which results in them sharing Christ's "heavenly flesh."

## Jesus Was Fully God and Fully Man

The clear and consistent teaching of Scripture is that Jesus was fully divine and fully human. This is a mystery which must be accepted by faith, for the Incarnation is the greatest miracle ever to occur. Although Jesus had no human father, He did have a human mother. He was both the Son of God and the Son of Man.

The first prophecy of the coming Messiah is found in Genesis 3:15. According to this promise, the Messiah would be the "seed of the woman." The Hebrew word translated "seed" (*zerah*) means "descendant." Those who teach that Jesus had "heavenly flesh" and thus did not descend from Eve protest that a woman does not have "seed." They misunderstand the meaning of *zerah*. God Himself declared that the One who would crush the head of the serpent would be a descendant of Eve. For Him to be her descendant, He had to be a genuine human being.

The Messiah was also to be the "seed of Abraham" (Genesis 22:18; Galatians 3:16). This means He would be Abraham's descendant. He would also be from the tribe of Judah (Genesis 49:10-12). He would be "made of the seed of David according to the flesh" (Romans 1:3; Psalm 132:11; Luke 1:32), but He would descend from David through David's son Nathan, not through Solomon and thus through Jeconiah (Jeremiah 22:28-30; Luke 3:31).

These Scriptures, and many others, indicate that Jesus shared completely in everything inherently involved in human existence. The word "flesh" (Greek, *sarx*) does not mean "skin"; it means "human nature." Thus Jesus, like any human being, had a human body, soul, spirit, mind, heart, and everything else required to be a real human being. Only by becoming fully human could He redeem us. Jesus received His human nature from Mary; otherwise He could not truly be called the "seed of David." Mary was no mere surrogate mother, no incubator into whose womb

God placed a new human nature which never existed anywhere before. Jesus stands in solidarity with the human race because He was "made of a woman" (Galatians 4:4). The word translated "of" (Greek, *ek*) means that Jesus received His humanity from Mary.

The only way Jesus differed from us is that He did not possess the sin nature. By the miracle of the virgin birth and by the fact that He was begotten by the Holy Spirit, He was spared the sin nature. But this does not make Him any less human than us, for the sin nature is not inherent to human nature. Both Adam and Eve were complete human beings before they sinned, and thus before they possessed the sin nature. Jesus is the last Adam (I Corinthians 15:45). Like the first Adam, He had no sin. But unlike the first Adam, Jesus never did sin, and thus He avoided being contaminated by the sin nature. (See Hebrews 2:17; 4:15; II Corinthians 5:21.)

Some may question how Jesus could have possessed a genuine human nature if He had no human father. But Adam had no human father, and he was a genuine human being. For that matter, neither did Eve have a human father. Jesus had a human mother and therefore must be a genuine and complete human being. His deity was contributed by the Holy Spirit. How this could be is a mystery because it is a miracle. The human mind cannot explain any miracle, much less the greatest miracle ever to occur. We accept by faith what Scripture says about Jesus: He is God, and He is man. When we have exhausted everything we can say about Him, we leave the rest with God. It is the privilege of the Sovereign Lord to do what He wishes to do without consulting with or explaining it to human beings.

According to Hebrews 1:9, human beings are the Messiah's "fellows." It may be suggested that the Son's "fellows" or peers are angels, and that this is a reference to His superior anointing beyond that given to the angels. But for this to be true, the angels would have to in some way be the Son's peers, or equals. They are not; He is superior to them in every way. The only way the Son can be said to have peers is in the Incarnation; He took on genuine humanity, thus declaring His solidarity with the human race. (See Hebrews 2:17.) In Hebrews 3:14, the same Greek word translated "fellows" here (*metochous*) is used to describe the way in which believers are identified with Christ.

Hebrews 2:10 declares, "For it became him, for whom are all things, and by whom are all things, in bringing many sons unto glory, to make the captain of their salvation perfect through sufferings." In view of Jesus' sinlessness (Romans 8:3; Hebrews 4:15), the idea that He was made "perfect through sufferings" may seem strange. Jesus was morally perfect from His conception in Mary's womb onward. The word "perfect" is translated from a form of the Greek *teleios*, which has to do with maturity or completeness. The idea here is the same as that in Luke 2:52, where it is recorded that the boy Jesus "increased in wisdom and stature, and in favor with God and men." Moral perfection is not in view, but the genuineness of the Messiah's humanity is. Jesus shared in the full range of human experiences, including temptation. (See Hebrews 2:18; 4:15.) He was made "perfect" or complete in relation to His humanity by participating fully in the human condition, including suffering. (See Hebrews 5:8-9.)

By means of the Incarnation, Jesus identifies so completely with human beings that He and they "are all of one" (Hebrews 2:11). Thus there can be no difference between Jesus' humanity and that of the human race at large, except His exemption from the sin nature. Because He stands in absolute solidarity with the human race, "He is not ashamed to call them brethren" (Hebrews 2:11). The marvel of the redemptive plan is that in order to "bring many sons to glory (Hebrews 2:10), God was willing to stoop to become one of us. (See Philippians 2:5-8.) Since we could not come to Him, He came to us.

In Hebrews 2:12, the writer of Hebrews quotes the Septuagint translation of Psalm 22:22. In this Messianic Psalm (poetic prophecy about the coming Messiah), which by definition addresses the Messiah's humanity, not His deity, He is seen declaring His solidarity with the human race even to the point of lifting up His voice in praise to God "in the midst of the assembly," or in the same way that human beings lift up their voices as they assemble to praise God.

It is essential to note here that the Messiah's conversation with God arises from His human nature, not from His deity. This is demanded by a reading of Psalm 22. (See, for example, Psalm 22:9-10.) This is not a picture of one divine person speaking to another, but of a genuinely human Messiah speaking to God just as surely as any human being would.

The writer's point in quoting Psalm 22:22 is to reinforce and demonstrate the identification of the Messiah with His human peers ("My brethren"), a theme which has continued since Hebrews 1:9. The phrase "in the midst of the church" underscores His identification with those who assemble to praise God; He is one of them so completely that He joins them in praising God. This offers insight as to the nature of the prayers of Jesus. (See Hebrews 5:7.) They do not illustrate conversations between persons in the Godhead, nor were they a mere charade. They serve to demonstrate the Messiah's full participation in human existence; if He had no need for prayer, He would not have been human.

According to Hebrews 2:17, the Messiah's identification with human beings is complete: "Wherefore in all things it behoved him to be made like unto his brethren, that he might be a merciful and faithful high priest in things pertaining to God, to make reconciliation for the sins of the people." He was made like us "in all things." The Incarnation was necessary so Jesus could function as "a merciful and faithful High Priest." The "High Priest" concept requires complete identification of the priest with those he represents. A priest could represent only those with whom he stood in solidarity. (See Hebrews 2:14-18; 4:15; 5:7-10.) Like the high priest under the Levitical system, the Messiah was like his brethren as to His humanity, but unlike the Levitical high priest, the Messiah brought God and man together.

In the Incarnation, the deity of Jesus did not override, obscure, or overwhelm His humanity. It did not prevent Him from sympathizing with our weaknesses or from being tempted as we are: "For we have not an high priest which cannot be touched with the feeling of our infirmities; but was in all points tempted like as we are, yet without sin" (Hebrews 4:15).

The genuineness of Jesus' prayers is seen in Hebrews 5:7: "Who in the days of his flesh, when he had offered up prayers and supplications with strong crying and tears unto him that was able to save him from death, and was heard in that he feared." Those who deny the complete solidarity of Jesus with humanity have suggested that His prayers did not arise out of any real need to pray, but that they were merely examples for us to follow. Thus the humanity of the Messiah is reduced from any meaningful identification with human beings (in contradiction to Hebrews 2:14, 17) to a mere moral influence. His prayers, according to this view, were simply a charade, a well-intentioned drama in which Jesus *acted* as if He needed divine assistance even though He did not.

But the prayers of Jesus were genuine, springing out of the fullness of His humanity. "He ... offered up prayers and supplications, with vehement cries and tears to Him who was able to save Him from death, and was heard because of His godly fear." This was done "in the days of His flesh." To say, "in the days of His flesh," "emphasizes the conditions of human weakness of which He partook during His earthly life and ... does not imply that His incarnate state was terminated with His exaltation to the right hand of God. If the expression did have this meaning, it would seriously weaken [the] argument that Christians have right now a high priest who feels for them and with them in all their temptations and sorrows."[2] It would also indicate that the Incarnation was not genuine, for genuine humanity cannot be discarded and cease to exist. The NEB translates the phrase, "In the days of his earthly life."

Jesus "offered up" (the same root word is used in Hebrews 5:1 of the gifts and sacrifices the high priest offered under the Law) both prayers (Greek, *deēseis*) and supplications (Greek,

---

[2] F.F. Bruce, *The New International Commentary on the New Testament, The Epistle to the Hebrews* (Grand Rapids, MI: Wm. B. Eerdmans Publishing Co., 1964), 98.

*hiketērias*). *Deēsis* (from which *deēseis* comes) is used exclusively in the New Testament of entreaties addressed to God. *Hiketērias* is derived from *hikesia* and is used only here in the New Testament. When a word appears only once in Scripture (this is called by Greek grammarians a *hapax legomenon*), it is sometimes difficult to determine its exact meaning because there is so little contextual evidence. But the word is used by a very early Christian writer to refer to eager supplication (I Clement 59:2).[3] An examination of the prayers of Jesus indicates that they occurred in a variety of contexts. Some were simply entreaties addressed to God for various purposes. (See Matthew 11:25-27; Mark 1:35; 6:46; Luke 3:21; 5:16; 6:12; 9:18; John 11:41-42; 17.) But there were times when the prayers of Jesus went beyond this and could be classified as "eager" or even desperate supplications. (See Luke 22:41-44; Matthew 27:46.) This is apparently what the writer of Hebrews has in mind, for he identifies these prayers and supplications as being made "with vehement cries and tears."

That the prayers of Jesus were genuine is further underscored by the fact that they were "offered up ... to Him who was able to save Him from death." In the prayers which arose out of His genuine humanity, Jesus prayed "to Him," or to God. This was not, as is suggested by some, a case of one divine person praying to another divine person. Such an idea violates the radical monotheism of Scripture and would be difficult to distinguish from ditheism (a belief in two gods). It would also indicate a subordination of the divine person praying to the divine person prayed to, making the first somehow inferior to the second. But neither, as others suggest, were the prayers of Jesus a case of our Lord praying to Himself. Jesus possessed a complete human psyche by means of which He communicated with other people and with God just as any human being does. Since He is

---

[3] Walter Bauer, *A Greek-English Lexicon of the New Testament and Other Early Christian Literature*, trans. and adapted by William F. Arndt and F. Wilbur Gingrich, rev. and augmented by F. Wilbur Gingrich and Frederick W. Danker, 2nd ed. (Chicago: University of Chicago Press, 1979), 374.

unique in that He is both God and man, there is no satisfactory way to explain this in terms completely understandable to the finite minds of men. There may, however, be a vague parallel in the way human beings can consult with themselves from different points of view.

Included, apparently, in the prayers in view in this verse are those in the Garden of Gethsemane, when Jesus prayed, "O My Father, if it is possible, let this cup pass from Me" (Matthew 26:39). Though God was able to save Him from death, and though Jesus "was heard because of His godly fear," Jesus experienced the death of the cross. This is because Jesus' cry to be saved from death did not terminate His prayer. He concluded, "Nevertheless, not as I will, but as You will" (Matthew 26:39). The atonement which would issue from Christ's death was the will of God; there was no escaping the cross. That Jesus would actually pray these words indicates further the completeness of His human nature: He had a human will which He subordinated to the will of God. If this had been the case of one divine person praying to another, it would mean that the will of one was opposed to the will of the other. There is, however, no bifurcation in the will of God. (See Ephesians 1:5, 11.) Not even those who believe God exists as three persons would suggest that He exists as a divine committee where there is the possibility of one person having a will different than the others. When Jesus prayed, "Nevertheless, not as I will," He spoke from His human nature, indicating that, as a man, He abhorred what was to come. It was not so much the physical pain He dreaded, but the shameful experience of dying a death deserved by a sinner (Hebrews 12:2). Jesus had never sinned, but He would die just as if He had, so that we, who had done no righteousness, could live just as if we had. (See II Corinthians 5:21; Romans 5:12-21.)

The word translated "godly fear" is *eulabeias*, from *eulabeia*, which is a compound word formed from *eu* and *lambano*. *Lambano* means to take in the sense of receiving. When coupled with *eu*, the idea is to take hold well, carefully, surely, cautiously. *Eulabeia* is also found in Hebrews 12:28: "Therefore, since we are receiving a kingdom which cannot be

18

shaken, let us have grace, by which we may serve God acceptably with reverence and godly fear." As it pertains to one's relationship with God, *eulabeia* means to be careful and cautious in reverencing Him. This was perfectly exemplified in the life of Jesus. God hears the prayers of those who sincerely reverence Him.

Hebrews 5:8 continues to focus on the humanity of Jesus: "Though he were a Son, yet learned he obedience by the things which he suffered." Hebrews points out that even though Jesus was the Son of God, and thus superior to the Aaronic priests, to Joshua, to Moses, to the angels, and to the prophets of old, He nevertheless "learned obedience by the things which He suffered." It would be incredible to think this statement pertains in any way to His deity. God is omniscient; there is nothing for Him to learn. God is sovereign; there is no one for Him to obey. But as it pertains to His humanity, Jesus experienced all that any human being experiences, including the painful experiences by which one matures in life. (See Hebrews 2:18.)

## Response to "His Heavenly Flesh"

At this point, I will respond to the teaching that Jesus did not share in our human nature, but that He had "heavenly flesh." The response will take the form of printing out the Scripture to which the notes I received refer, followed by the interpretation of the Scripture given in the notes (this will be enclosed in a box), and then an explanation of the actual teaching of the Scripture. The Scripture given in the notes will be from the King James Version. Unless otherwise indicated, my comments use the New King James Version.[4]

"All flesh is not the same flesh: but there is one kind of flesh of men, another flesh of beasts,

---

[4] *The Holy Bible, The New King James Version* (Nashville, TN: Broadman & Holman Publishers, 1982).

19

another of fishes, and another of birds" (I
Corinthians 15:39).

| "All flesh is not the same." |
| --- |

It is true that I Corinthians 15:39 declares that all flesh is not
the same. But there is no indication in this verse that there is such
a thing as "heavenly flesh." This is very important, because if
there is no such thing as "heavenly flesh," the entire teaching
collapses. All that this verse teaches is that human flesh is not the
same as the flesh of beasts or of fish or of birds. Indeed, since
"there is one kind of flesh of men," if Jesus was a man – and He
was – this means that He had the same kind of flesh as we do.
This is denied by the "heavenly flesh" teaching.

"There are also celestial bodies, and bodies
terrestrial: but the glory of the celestial is one, and
the glory of the terrestrial is another" (I
Corinthians 15:40).

| "There are earthly bodies and heavenly bodies different from each other in glory." |
| --- |

There is still no claim that there is such a thing as "heavenly
flesh." The "celestial bodies" include the sun, the moon, and the
stars (I Corinthians 15:41). The "bodies terrestrial" include those
of men, beasts, fishes and birds (I Corinthians 15:39).

"The first man is of the earth, earthy: the second
man is the Lord from heaven" (I Corinthians
15:47).

| "The Adamic man is created from earth (dust). The Second Adam, Christ, is not earthy but the Lord from heaven." |
| --- |

This verse does not say that Jesus did not have a physical body made from the dust of the earth, as did Adam. It simply says that the second man "is the Lord from heaven." In other words, Jesus is the Lord, and He came down from heaven. We learn elsewhere that the means by which He came down from heaven was to take on genuine human existence as a man; He was God manifest "in the flesh" (I Timothy 3:16). He was the Word "made flesh" (John 1:14). Indeed, John wrote, "Hereby know ye the Spirit of God: Every spirit that confesseth that Jesus Christ is come in the flesh is of God: And every spirit that confesseth not that Jesus Christ is come in the flesh is not of God: and this is that spirit of antichrist, whereof ye have heard that it should come; and even now already is it in the world" (I John 4:2-3). John wrote in opposition to incipient Gnosticism, which declared that Jesus did not have genuine human existence. This false teaching said that Jesus only appeared to be human, which is quite similar to the "heavenly flesh" teaching.

In I Corinthians 15, Paul is discussing the resurrection from the dead and the fact that it will be a bodily resurrection. In the resurrection, the corruptible human body will be made incorruptible (I Corinthians 15:42, 52-54). The natural body that believers now possess will, in the resurrection, be made a spiritual body (I Corinthians 15:44). This does not mean it will be a *spirit* body; it will be a *spiritual* body. That is, it will be a real body which includes flesh and bones (Luke 24:39), but it will be uniquely adapted to life in the realm of the spirit, just as our present body is adapted to life in the physical realm.

In I Corinthians 15:45, Paul wrote, "And so it is written, The first man Adam was made a living soul; the last Adam was made a quickening spirit." This does not mean that Jesus has a "spirit body" or "heavenly flesh." It means that Jesus, as God, is a life-giving Spirit. (See Philippians 1:19.)

I Corinthians 15:46 asserts: "Howbeit that was not first which is spiritual, but that which is natural; and afterward that which is spiritual." This simply means that the natural, corruptible human body precedes the incorruptible, spiritual body which is obtained in the resurrection.

"As is the earthy, such are they also that are earthy: and as is the heavenly, such are they also that are heavenly" (I Corinthians 15:48).

> "The new birth translates us from the earthy man to the heavenly man."

The implication of this statement in the larger context of the "heavenly flesh" teaching is that when we are born again, we somehow are transformed from having earthly, corruptible flesh to having incorruptible, heavenly flesh. This is not the meaning of this verse. This simply means that prior to the resurrection, human beings have "earthy" bodies; after the resurrection, they will have "heavenly" bodies. The earthy bodies are the natural, weak, corruptible bodies; the heavenly bodies are the spiritual, powerful, incorruptible bodies. (See I Corinthians 15:42-44.)

Interestingly, the notes avoid I Corinthians 15:49, which declares, "And as we have borne the image of the earthy, we shall also bear the image of the heavenly." This verse makes it exceedingly clear that we do *not* yet bear the image of the heavenly, which is exactly contrary to the "heavenly flesh" teaching. We *shall* bear it, but we do not now. Paul's point is that prior to the resurrection, "we have borne the image of the earthy," but in the resurrection, "we shall also bear the image of the heavenly." This has not yet occurred.

"Now this I say, brethren, that flesh and blood cannot inherit the kingdom of God; neither doth corruption inherit incorruption" (I Corinthians 15:50).

> "The flesh and blood of the first Adam will not inherit the kingdom of God."

The "heavenly flesh" teaching takes this to mean that if a person is born again, he or she no longer has corruptible flesh and blood. That is not the meaning of the verse. In the context of I Corinthians 15, the "kingdom of God" refers to the resurrection. As the following verses explain, this verse means that in order to go up in the resurrection, believers will "be changed" (I Corinthians 15:51, 52) by being "raised incorruptible" (I Corinthians 15:52). This will happen when the "corruptible" puts on "incorruption" and the "mortal" puts on "immortality" (I Corinthians 15:53-54).

> "Know ye not that your bodies are the members of Christ? shall I then take the members of Christ, and make them the members of an harlot? God forbid" (I Corinthians 6:15).

"Our bodies are now members of His heavenly body."

This verse does *not* say that our bodies are members of Christ's "heavenly body." It does not even say that Christ has a "heavenly body." The language is obviously metaphorical, like that of I Corinthians 12:12-17, where the various individuals who are in the church are compared to the members of the human body in their function. All that this means is that we belong to Christ. If the "heavenly flesh" teaching were true, this verse would suggest that by means of committing fornication with a believer, a harlot could somehow partake of the "heavenly body." Paul's point here is clear: Since we belong to Christ, we cannot commit fornication. The verse says nothing about the nature of the believer's human body.

> "For as many of you as have been baptized into Christ have put on Christ" (Galatians 3:27).

"When we are baptized, we put on Christ, the heavenly man."

Here, the teaching adds words to Scripture. Paul did not say that when we are baptized we "put on Christ, the heavenly man." He said that when we are baptized into Christ, we "have put on Christ." This has nothing to do with the body Jesus obtained in the resurrection. It simply means that by means of baptism in the name of Jesus Christ we are identified with Christ; we are united with Him. There is absolutely no biological change that occurs when we are baptized.

> "Therefore if any man be in Christ, he is a new creature: old things are passed away; behold, all things are become new" (II Corinthians 5:17).

"We are a new creation because we have put on Christ, the heavenly man."

Again, the teaching adds the words "the heavenly man." This verse has nothing to do with any change in the believer's physical body. As II Corinthians 5:21 points out, this means that believers are "made the righteousness of God in him." The "old things" are the sins in which we previously lived.

> "And the Word was made flesh, and dwelt among us, (and we beheld his glory, the glory as of the only begotten of the Father,) full of grace and truth" (John 1:14).

"The flesh of the heavenly man is not from earthy substance but from the divine word become flesh."

The interpretation of this verse assumes that there is some kind of flesh other than that shared by human beings, a "heavenly flesh." This is not true. As I Corinthians 15:39 points out, there is only "one kind of flesh of men." There is no "heavenly flesh." If Jesus is the Word made flesh – and He is – He is the Word made *human* flesh, for the only other kinds of flesh which exist are the flesh of beasts, fish, and birds. John 1:14 does *not* say that the Word is "not from earthy substance."

> "That which was from the beginning, which we have heard, which we have seen with our eyes, which we have looked upon, and our hands have handled, of the Word of life" (I John 1:1).

> "Our hands 'handled' the Word of life as it manifested as the flesh of the sinless Lamb of God."

There is nothing in this verse to support the "heavenly flesh" teaching. The Word had no flesh until the Incarnation; as John 1:14 points out, the Word was "made flesh."

> "And without controversy great is the mystery of godliness: God was manifest in the flesh, justified in the Spirit, seen of angels, preached unto the Gentiles, believed on in the world, received up into glory" (I Timothy 3:16).

> "The flesh of the heavenly man is from God."

This interpretation has no basis in I Timothy 3:16. Nothing in the verse suggests that "the flesh of the heavenly man is from God." It is clear that the word "flesh" here has reference to Jesus' human existence, for it was "in the flesh" that He was "justified in the Spirit, seen of angels, preached unto the Gentiles, believed on in the world," and "received up into glory." "Heavenly flesh" would have no need of justification. Even in the resurrection, Jesus had human flesh (Luke 24:39), although it was incorruptible.

> "Take heed therefore unto yourselves, and to all the flock, over the which the Holy Ghost hath made you overseers, to feed the church of God,

which he hath purchased with his own blood"
(Acts 20:28).

> "The blood of the heavenly man is referred to as 'God's blood.' "

This verse means only that Jesus was God, and that thus His blood was the blood of God. If the "heavenly flesh" teaching is correct, Jesus cannot inherit the kingdom of God, for "flesh and blood cannot inherit the kingdom of God" (I Corinthians 15:50), and Jesus had blood.

> "Whereby are given unto us exceeding great and precious promises: that by these ye might be partakers of the divine nature, having escaped the corruption that is in the world through lust" (II Peter 1:4).

> "We are partakers of the divine nature in the heavenly man (body of Christ)."

The "heavenly flesh" teaching makes this verse say something it does not say. It does not say that we are partakers of the divine nature *in the heavenly man*; it says we might be partakers of the divine nature by means of the *exceeding great and precious promises*. This means that the wonderful promises of God enable us to share in the life of God by means of the indwelling Spirit (Romans 8:9; Galatians 2:20). If the "heavenly flesh" teaching is true, believers actually become divine.

> "For no man ever yet hated his own flesh; but nourisheth and cherisheth it, even as the Lord the church: For we are members of his body, of his flesh, and of his bones" (Ephesians 5:29-30).

> "The saints are His own (heavenly) flesh. We are now members of His heavenly body, flesh, and bones."

As with I Corinthians 6:15, above, this is metaphorical language. Paul does not mean that believers have literally become the body of Jesus; He means they are intimately related to Him by means of the new birth. This metaphorical language continues into the next verse, where a husband and wife are said to be "one flesh." This does not mean they somehow share in a common body; the point has to do with their intimacy. If believers have "heavenly flesh," why do they need to eat, drink, or sleep? Why do they suffer pain and die? And, most telling of all, why does their body decay and corrupt when they die?

> "For this cause shall a man leave his father and mother, and shall be joined unto his wife, and they two shall be one flesh. This is a great mystery: but I speak concerning Christ and the church" (Ephesians 5:31-32).

"Being one flesh in marriage is a mystery type referring to the union of the heavenly flesh in the new birth."

There is nothing about "heavenly flesh" in this passage. The "great mystery" which is illustrated by the intimacy of the husband and wife is the intimate relationship which exists between Christ and the church. There is no "union of the heavenly flesh." There is simply a union of believers with Jesus Christ by means of His indwelling Spirit.

> "That which is born of the flesh is flesh; and that which is born of the Spirit is spirit" (John 3:6).

"That which is born of (earthy, Adamic) flesh is (earthy, Adamic) flesh."

Again, there is nothing about "heavenly flesh" here. Jesus simply means that the natural birth produces human beings, while the new birth affects only the spirit of man. Indeed,

27

contrary to the "heavenly flesh" teaching, the birth of the Spirit has no effect on the flesh at all. If "spirit" means "heavenly flesh" here, then Jesus Himself did not have "heavenly flesh," for He said, after His resurrection, "Behold my hands and my feet, that it is I myself: handle me, and see; for a spirit hath not flesh and bones, as ye see me have" (Luke 24:39). Jesus denied being a "spirit"; He claimed to have "flesh and bones." There is no hint this was "heavenly" flesh and bones.

> "And you, being dead in your sins and the uncircumcision of your flesh, hath he quickened together with him, having forgiven you all trespasses" (Colossians 2:13).

---

"The unsaved man is dead because of (1) the sin and (2) the uncircumcision of the (Adamic, earthy) flesh."

---

Spiritual death is separation from fellowship with God. It is to be cut off from spiritual life. But there is nothing in this verse to support the "heavenly flesh" teaching. If the "heavenly flesh" teaching is true, all men who have previously been uncircumcised would be miraculously circumcised upon being born again!

> "For all flesh is as grass, and all the glory of man as the flower of grass. The grass withereth, and the flower thereof falleth away" (I Peter 1:24).

---

"All flesh is as grass, except the flesh of the new man, the Second Adam, Christ."

---

As is typical of false teaching, the "heavenly flesh" doctrine continues to add to the Word of God. I Peter 1:24 does *not* say all flesh is as grass *except the flesh of the new man*. In this quote from Isaiah 40:6-8, Peter is simply pointing out in metaphorical language the transitory nature of human beings as opposed to the permanence of the Word of the Lord (I Peter 1:25). Peter does not intend to make any statement about the biological nature of human flesh. Just as grass withers, the glory of human beings is temporary.

> "For thou wilt not leave my soul in hell; neither wilt thou suffer thine Holy One to see corruption" (Psalm 16:10).

> "And it shall come to pass in the last days, saith God, I will pour out of my Spirit upon all flesh: and your sons and your daughters shall prophesy, and your young men shall see visions, and your old men shall dream dreams ... He seeing this before spake of the resurrection of Christ, that his soul was not left in hell, neither his flesh did see corruption" (Acts 2:27, 31).

> "Wherefore he saith also in another psalm, Thou shalt not suffer thine Holy One to see corruption" (Acts 13:35).

---

"The Second Adam, Christ, shall not see corruption of His flesh."

---

It is true that the human body of Jesus did not corrupt. But this was not because He had incorruptible, "heavenly flesh." It was because He was resurrected from the dead before His body could decay and corrupt. These verses actually prove just the opposite of what the "heavenly flesh" teaching asserts. They point out that because of the prophecy that his flesh would not see corruption, Jesus was resurrected from the dead. In fact, Acts 13:34 declares, "And as concerning that he raised him up from the dead, now *no more to return to corruption* ...." The body of Jesus was facing corruption, but it was avoided by the resurrection.

"Forasmuch as ye know that ye were not redeemed with corruptible things, as silver and gold, from your vain conversation received by tradition from your fathers; But with the precious blood of Christ, as of a lamb without blemish and without spot" (I Peter 1:18-19).

"Take heed therefore unto yourselves, and to all the flock, over the which the Holy Ghost hath made you overseers, to feed the church of God, which he hath purchased with his own blood" (Acts 20:28).

"The blood (of the Second Adam, Christ) that redeemed us declared *incorruptible* and *precious*. This is not true of the blood of the first Adam."

Grammatically, I Peter 1:18-19 does not say that the blood of Jesus was not corruptible. The word "corruptible" is an adjective which modifies the nouns "silver" and "gold," not "blood." The "heavenly flesh" teaching declares that only the blood of Jesus is precious, but Psalm 72:14 proves that even the blood of the poor and needy is precious. Although blood is corruptible, it is still precious.

As we noted above, Acts 20:28 simply proves that Jesus is God. Thus everything that belongs to Him belongs to God, including His blood. It does not say that the blood of Jesus was incorruptible.

"Wherefore when he cometh into the world, he saith, Sacrifice and offering thou wouldest not, but a body hast thou prepared me" (Hebrews 10:5).

"Who verily was foreordained before the foundation of the world, but was manifest in these last times for you" (I Peter 1:20).

> "Prophecy declared an especially prepared heavenly body for sacrifice offering."

Neither of these verses suggests that the body of Jesus was "heavenly." In Hebrews 10:5-7, the writer of Hebrews offers a form of the Septuagint version of Psalm 40:6-8, which is itself "an interpretative paraphrase of the Hebrew text."[5] This is not unprecedented in the Book of Hebrews; the Septuagint, or a form of it, is frequently appealed to make the author's point. There is no problem here concerning the integrity of Scripture; the writer of Hebrews was inspired of God in his use of the Septuagint or any variation of it.

This Incarnation is the topic in this passage. The quote from psalms has to do with what the Messiah said to God in conjunction with His entrance into the world. It is not a communication between persons in the Godhead prior to the Incarnation. The word translated "cometh" in the KJV (Greek, *eiserchomenos*) is a present tense participle which functions in the active voice. The KJV translation of this word ("cometh") is more precise than that of the NKJV ("came"). The idea in *eiserchomenos* is "coming." The verb *legei* is translated "he saith" by the KJV, which again is more accurate than the "He said" of the NKJV. *Legei* is the third person singular present active indicative form of *legō* and should be translated "he says" or "he is saying." This is the idea in the Old English "saith."

When did the Messiah make this statement? The KJV reads, "When he cometh into the world, he saith ...." In today's English, this means, "When he is coming into the world, he is saying ...." This suggests that the Messiah made this statement shortly after the assumption of His human nature, perhaps at His birth, since the phrase "coming into the world" is a Jewish expression for

---

[5] Bruce, *The Epistle to the Hebrews,* 232.

birth.[6] But this is problematic in view of the questions concerning the development of the Messiah's human consciousness. If He experienced human existence as do all other human beings – and that is what Scripture declares – His human consciousness developed. This is strongly indicated in Luke 2:52. Thus, the Messiah did not have a fully aware human consciousness at birth to enable Him to make a statement like this.

Actually, the word "when" does not appear in the Greek text of Hebrews 10:5, and this may help resolve the question. The verse itself does not indicate precisely when this statement was made. The present participle "coming" (Greek, *eiserchomenos*) does indicate it could not have been prior to the Incarnation, as does the present active "He says" (Greek, *legei*). But since *legei* can be understood as a "timeless present"[7] and the word "when" is absent, we may assume that this statement was simply made by the Messiah at some point after the Incarnation. A literal translation would be, "Therefore, coming (or 'entering') the world, He says ...." The statement "a body hast thou prepared me" indicates strongly that the entire quote was made after the Incarnation when the Messiah was existing in the body so prepared. The word *katertiso*, translated "hast thou prepared" by the KJV, is in the aorist tense, which indicates it is something accomplished in the past. Since the body was already prepared, and since this statement was made in conjunction with the Incarnation, it could theoretically have been made by the Messiah at any time during His life on earth prior to His crucifixion.

This communication between the Messiah and God should be understood in the same sense as all the prayers of Jesus. The idea here is not that of a conversation between two divine persons, but of a genuinely human Messiah communicating with

---

[6] Paul Ellingworth, *New International Greek Testament Commentary, Commentary on Hebrews* (Grand Rapids, MI: Wm. B. Eerdmans Publishing Co., 1993), 500.

[7] Ellingworth, *Commentary on Hebrews*, 500.

32

God from His human psyche, which He possessed as surely as a human body, as Hebrews 10:5 indicates, and whose mission was to do the will of God (Hebrews 10:7). In the mystery of the Incarnation, the Messiah was, of course, the brightness of God's glory and the express image of God's person. But His deity did not obscure or overwhelm His humanity; the nature of the Incarnation was to somehow manifest God in human existence. (See John 1:14; I Timothy 3:16.) This, the greatest of miracles, will forever remain a mystery, as are all miracles. Since Scripture does not tell us precisely how the Incarnation worked, all we can do is confess all that the Scripture does have to say to be true, both as to Christ's deity and humanity. When we attempt to fit the declarations of Scripture on this subject into a logical structure allowing no contradictions, we will inevitably cloud or confuse either the deity or the humanity of Christ. It should be enough to say that Jesus was both God and man.

Since the Incarnation involved God emptying Himself (Philippians 2:7, where the Greek *heauton ekenōsen* which is translated "made himself of no reputation" by the KJV but more properly means "emptied Himself") not by giving up anything, including His deity, but by "taking the form of a bondservant, and coming in the likeness of men," we must confess that there is some way in which Jesus is the "human face of God."

The same word used to say that Jesus existed in the "form" of God (*morphē*)[8] is used to say that He took the "form" of a

---

[8] In Philippians 2:6, the word translated "form" (Greek, *morphē*) lacks a precise equivalent in the English language. Its connection with "form" or "shape" doesn't usually have to do with what is external but with what is truly indicative of the essence of a thing. As Fee points out in his excellent and thorough discussion of *morphē,* the word indicates "those characteristics and qualities that are essential to it. Hence, it means *that which truly characterizes a given reality*" (Gordon D. Fee, *Pauline Christology: An Exegetical-Theological Study* [Peabody, MA: Hendrickson Publishers, 2007], 378). The word "being" (Greek, *hyparchon*) is a participle which indicates continual existence. The word translated "robbery" (Greek, *harpagmon*) in the KJV is somewhat of a puzzle, since it appears only here in New Testament Greek, nowhere in the Septuagint, and rarely in secular Greek. Fee offers two possible views, both with the same outcome. First, *harpagmos* "is not to be

bondservant. In other words, He "took on the 'essential quality' of what it meant to be a slave."[9] Genuine, authentic, and full humanity was included in the essential quality. To say that Jesus was made in the likeness (*homoiōma*) of men does not mean that Jesus merely had an external appearance of being human but that He was really something less than human. The plural word "men" (*anthrōpōn*) means that Jesus was human. The fact that He was in the likeness of human beings means that although He was human, He was not only human; He was also God.[10]

The language of Philippians 2:6-8 indicates the genuineness of Christ's humanity. His humanity was so complete that He experienced all that is common to man, including the need to pray and commune with God. How He could *be* God and yet pray is an enigma, but it is one we must accept. To attempt the resolve the tension this presents by suggesting that Jesus is a second person in the Godhead praying to the first person solves nothing and creates new problems. This does not explain why one divine person would need to pray to another or how such prayers could be valid. It does not explain how one divine person could honestly say to another, "Not My will, but Yours, be done" (Luke 22:42). If it is thought that the radical monotheism of Scripture (see Deuteronomy 6:4) permits the one God to exist as two or three distinct but completely equal persons, how could one confess to have a different desire or will than another? For that matter, how could one say to another, "I have come ... to do Your will, O God"? (Hebrews 10:7).

---

thought of as a 'thing' at all . . . ; rather, it is an abstract noun, emphasizing the concept of 'grasping' or 'seizing.' Thus, Christ did not consider 'equality with God' to consist of 'grasping' or being 'selfish'; rather, he rejected this popular view of kingly power by 'pouring himself out' for the sake of others" (Fee, *Pauline Christology*, 382). The second view is that *harpagmos* is "a synonym of its cognate [*harpagma*] ("booty" or "prey"), which . . . denotes something like 'a matter to be seized upon,' in the sense of 'taking advantage of it.' . . . Thus . . . the true God-likeness that is found in Christ's mind-set has revealed God to be self-giving rather than self-serving, loving rather than exploiting" (Fee, *Pauline Christology*, 383).

[9] Fee, *Pauline Christology*, 385.

[10] Fee, *Pauline Christology*, 388.

As inexplicable as it may be, the best way to think about the conversations between the Messiah and God is to attribute them to the genuineness and fullness of Christ's human existence. He was a man, so He shared fully in the experiences of man, including the need for prayer.

The Hebrew text of Psalm 40:6 reads "My ears you have opened" where the Septuagint has "a body hast thou prepared me." The Septuagint is an interpretive rendering, understanding the ears to be representative of the entire body. Literally, the Hebrew reads "My ears you have digged." This seems to be a reference to the idea of the creation of the human body, made from the earth (Genesis 2:7), in which the various orifices, including the ears, were "digged out." Thus, instead of proving that the Messiah had "heavenly flesh," this proves that He had a body like the first Adam. If the Messiah had a body, He would have ears. But it suits the purpose of the writer of Hebrews to quote the Septuagint, for his emphasis is on the body of the Messiah as the sacrifice which did what the sacrifices of the Law could not do.

> "Having therefore, brethren, boldness to enter into the holiest by the blood of Jesus, By a new and living way, which he hath consecrated for us, through the veil, that is to say, his flesh" (Hebrews 10:19-20).

"The flesh and blood of the earthy, Adamic man can not accomplish this; the *flesh* of the heavenly man is referred to here as the 'veil.' "

These verses say nothing about Jesus having "heavenly flesh." Because we have in Christ a High Priest who is seated at the right hand of the throne of the Majesty in the heavens (Hebrews 8:1), and because He is a High Priest who has completely satisfied the righteous judgment of God upon sin by the offering of His body (Hebrews 10:10-18), we can boldly enter the true Holiest place by His blood. The word "therefore" refers back to the discussion of the atoning work of Christ and reveals its logical effect. The death of Christ on the cross did nothing less than to make it possible for people of faith to be cleansed from their sins (Hebrews 10:22) and to be qualified to enter directly into the presence of God.

The statement that Christ consecrated this new and living way "through the veil, that is, His flesh" has been the subject of much speculation. Some have suggested that the point is that His flesh (i.e., human nature) was a veil which obscured His deity. But this seems to impose a meaning on the verse which is not self-evident. Rather, the language seems to continue the symbolism of Hebrews 10:19 and may allude to the rending of the veil in the temple at the moment of Christ's death (Matthew 27:51; Mark 15:38; Luke 23:45). In this sense, the veil is not viewed as a barrier to entry into the Holiest Place; the rent veil provided free passage into the Most Holy Place. Likewise, the flesh (i.e., "the body of Jesus Christ" [Hebrews 10:10]), pierced upon the cross, provides access into the true Holiest of All. The humanity of Jesus is not a barrier to intimacy with God, it is the means by which He stands in solidarity with us as our High Priest (Hebrews 10:21), thus enabling us to enter into the most intimate relationship with God.

If the reference to the veil here has no allusion to the rending of the temple veil, but if it refers simply to the function of the inner veil in the tabernacle in guarding the way to the Most Holy Place, the verse still indicates that it is through the flesh, or human nature, of Jesus that a way has been made into the presence of God. There still is no necessary idea of the veil as a barrier. On the Day of Atonement, it was no barrier. There was a legitimate provision for entry beyond the veil. Just as the veil opened a way into the Most Holy Place on the Day of Atonement, so the sacrifice of the body of Jesus Christ opened the way into the presence of God as He atoned for the sins of the world on the cross.

"Wherefore, my brethren, ye also are become dead to the law by the body of Christ; that ye should be married to another, even to him who is raised from the dead, that we should bring forth fruit unto God" (Romans 7:4).

> "We are 'married' (made one flesh) to the heavenly man, the body of Christ by the new birth."

There is nothing in this verse to suggest that Christ has "heavenly flesh" or that we share in "heavenly flesh" by virtue of our "marriage" to Him. Grammatically, there is no reference at all to what kind of flesh believers have or what kind of flesh Jesus has. The point of the verse is that just as a woman whose husband dies is freed from her covenant obligations to him, so believers who are in union with Christ have "become dead to the law." The death of Jesus Christ terminated the era of the Law's dominion (Romans 10:4), and those who identify with Him in His death (see Romans 6:3-5) are thereby released from obligation to the Law. It was necessary that they be released from obligation to the Law in this manner in order that they might "be married to another," Jesus Christ. The believer cannot be obligated to two covenants at once; there can be no mixing of covenants or dividing of loyalties. God intended marriage to be monogamous, and on the same basis only one of the two covenants can be in effect at the same time.

"For what the law could not do, in that it was weak through the flesh, God sending his own Son in the likeness of sinful flesh, and for sin, condemned sin in the flesh" (Romans 8:3).

> "The Son of God (the heavenly man) was sent 'in the likeness' of sinful flesh, but was not of that sinful, Adamic flesh Himself."

Though the Law of Moses was holy (7:12), it had an inherent weakness. It was weak "through the flesh," that is, it made no provision for the fact that human nature is marred by sin, and that human beings are thus incapable of attaining a standard of perfection by their own strength. What the Law of Moses could not do was to impute righteousness. What the Law could not do, God accomplished by means of the Incarnation. God sent His own Son in the *likeness* of sinful flesh. Although the flesh, or human nature, of Jesus was genuine humanity obtained from His human mother, Mary, Paul uses the word "likeness" because Jesus was spared the sin nature by virtue of the virgin birth. He had no human father; the Holy Spirit brought about His conception. If Paul had written that God sent His Son "in sinful flesh," he would have compromised the sinlessness of Christ. If he had written that God sent His son "in the likeness of flesh," he would have compromised the humanity of Christ. His wording is chosen precisely to communicate the true condition of the Incarnation: Jesus Christ is genuinely and completely human, but – like the first Adam [I Corinthians 15:45] – He did not possess the sin nature.

Jesus Christ, as God incarnate (I Timothy 3:16), is the Son of God sent into the world. (See John 3:17; 7:33; 17:18; 20:21; Galatians 4:4-6.) This does not mean He preexisted the Incarnation *as the Son*. He certainly did preexist the Incarnation, but *as the Word*. (See John 1:1-2, 14; I John 1:1-2.) John's use of "word" (*logos*) does not imply existence separate from God or even plurality of persons within God; John's use of "word" is reminiscent of Genesis 1, where God created by His word. God is the being of ultimate integrity, and His word cannot be separated from Him as having a conscience existence apart from Him, any more than the life of God can be separated from Him. In the Targums, Aramaic paraphrases of the Hebrew Scriptures, the word *memra*, Aramaic for "word," was used of God Himself. The fact that the Son was "sent" does not demand preexistence *as the Son* any more than the fact that John the Baptist was sent (John 1:6) implies his preexistence.

38

The Son of God was sent "on account of sin" (NKJV). His premier mission was redemption; Jesus came to solve the sin problem once and for all. (See John 1:29; I Corinthians 5:7; I John 2:2; Hebrews 10:12; Revelation 13:8.) Whereas sin had previously condemned all men, Jesus dealt with sin by turning the tables on it: He condemned sin. To condemn means to judge; Jesus provided the final judgment of sin on the Cross of Calvary. (See Colossians 2:14-15.) He did this "in the flesh," or in His genuine human existence. On the Cross, Jesus did not rely on His deity to in any way avoid the suffering associated with His substitutionary death. Although, on the Cross, He was God manifested in the flesh, just as He was and is at all points of His existence, through His humanity He humbled Himself to the point of death, and to the most despicable death known in the Roman Empire at the time, death on a cross. (See Philippians 2:8.)

The word translated "likeness" is *homoiōmati*, a form of the same word that is used in Philippians 2:7 to point out that Jesus was "made in the likeness of men." The word "likeness" does not compromise the genuineness and fullness of Christ's human nature. (See John 1:14; I Timothy 3:16; Hebrews 2:17.) In both Romans 8:3 and Philippians 2:7, Paul's emphasis is on what was visible to those who observed Jesus in His Incarnation. They could not see within Him to behold His complete human nature; they could, however, observe from external appearance that He was a man. It is possible that Paul used *homoiōma* in these instances to protect the doctrine of the Incarnation from the possibility of seeing Jesus as partaking of the sinful nature inherent in all other human beings. But it cannot mean that Jesus had "heavenly flesh" or that He was a "heavenly man."

"For I reckon that the sufferings of this present time are not worthy to be compared with the glory which shall be revealed in us" (Romans 8:18).

> "'The glory that shall be revealed in us' is the glory of the heavenly man, Christ."

Notice that this "glory" *shall* be revealed in us. It is something to be revealed in the future; it has not yet happened. The point of the verse is that though the believer identifies with Christ in His suffering (see Romans 8:17), this suffering – regardless of its intensity – will pale into insignificance when compared with the believer's ultimate identification with Christ in His glory. (See Philippians 3:21; Colossians 1:27; 3:4; Hebrews 2:10.)

Not all suffering experienced by the believer is due to identification with Christ. Some suffering is simply the consequence of living in a world marred by sin among people who are marred by sin. The suffering Paul has in mind here is that which comes upon a believer due to his faith in Christ. Perhaps the greatest example of this kind of suffering is the martyrdom of those who refuse to deny Christ even upon the threat of death. But even this will never be regretted by those who so testify to their faith in Christ; in the glorification, all suffering will be forgotten. This glorification will not occur until the second coming of Christ for His saints. (See Colossians 3:4; I John 3:2.)

> "For such an high priest became us, who is holy, harmless, undefiled, separate from sinners, and made higher than the heavens" (Hebrews 7:26).

> "The first man is of the earth, earthy: the second man is the Lord from heaven" (I Corinthians 15:47).

> "The first Adam is of the earth, earthy. The Second Adam is holy, undefiled, separate from sinners (separate from the first Adam) AND MADE HIGHER THAN THE HEAVENS. (Hallelujah!)"

We have already dealt with I Corinthians 15:47 above. It does *not* say that the second man, the Lord from heaven, did not have a human, earthy physical body. It simply means that the first Adam was exclusively human, while the Lord Jesus — though *also a man*, was divine as well. In fact, the context proves that Jesus *did* have a natural body: "So also is the resurrection of the dead. It is sown in corruption; it is raised in incorruption ... It is sown a natural body; it is raised a spiritual body ..." (I Corinthians 15:42, 44). Since Jesus was resurrected from the dead, this means His body too was "sown in corruption" and "raised in incorruption." It was "sown a *natural* body" and "raised a spiritual body." These verses apply to all who experience resurrection, including Jesus.

Hebrews 7:26 does not mean that Jesus had "heavenly flesh." The Incarnation uniquely suited Jesus to represent us as High Priest. (See Hebrews 2:14, 17-18; 4:15-16; 5:7-9.) Because He stands in complete solidarity with the human race, no man can complain that God does not understand our plight.

Jesus Christ is holy. The word "holy" is commonly translated from the Greek *hagios*, which has to do with separation, but in this case, the word is *hosios*. In the Septuagint, *hosios* is frequently used to translate the Hebrew *hasid*, which is related to the Hebrew *hesed*. *Hesed* means "loyal love" and is often used to indicate loyalty to covenant obligations. The significance here seems to be that Jesus loves us with a loyalty which is expressed in His faithful performance of all the conditions and promises of the New Covenant. The loyalty of His love is demonstrated upon Calvary's cross, to which He was willing to go even though it was distasteful to our sinless Savior to be made sin for us. (See Hebrews 12:2; Matthew 26:39; II Corinthians 5:21.)

Jesus Christ is harmless. The word translated "harmless" (Greek, *akakos*) is the negative form of *kakos*, which means "evil." *Akakos* means Jesus is not evil in any way. To translate the word "harmless" implies that He is incapable of doing harm, and that is certainly true. Some translations render the word "guileless," which means that Jesus is without cunning. He is

41

innocent not only of any inherent evil or wrongdoing, but also of any intent to do evil.

Jesus Christ is undefiled. Though He shared fully in human nature and lived on earth as a Man among men for more than three decades, and though He never shirked contact with sinners, He successfully resisted all defilement. (See Hebrews 4:15; Matthew 4:1.) Even though He was despised and rejected of men (Isaiah 53:3), no deceit was found in His mouth. Though He had committed no sin and was thus innocent, He did not revile those who reviled Him; He did not threaten those who caused His suffering. (See I Peter 2:22-23.) Men were disqualified for service under the Levitical priesthood by ritual defilements (see Leviticus 21:17-21). But there was nothing to disqualify Jesus from serving as the Great High Priest (see Hebrews 4:14).

Jesus Christ is separate from sinners. His human nature is genuine and complete. He was even made in the likeness of sinful flesh (Romans 8:3). He associated with sinners. (See Mark 2:16-17.) But He never once yielded to the temptation to sin. (See 4:15; I Peter 2:22; Matthew 4:1-11.) Thus, though He identifies completely with the human condition, He is separated from those who sin by His refusal to do so. To say Jesus was made in the likeness of sinful flesh preserves the genuineness of His humanity while rejecting any idea that He possessed the sin nature.[11]

Jesus Christ has become higher than the heavens. This is reminiscent of the declaration in Hebrews 1:3 that Jesus has "sat down at the right hand of the Majesty on high." Similar descriptions of the exaltation of Jesus are found elsewhere. (See Mark 16:19; Luke 22:69; Acts 2:33; 5:31; 7:55-56; Romans 8:34; Ephesians 1:20-22; Philippians 2:9; Colossians 3:1; Hebrews 10:12; 12:2; I Peter 3:22.) In none of these references is the idea

---

[11] Alternatively, the phrase "separate from sinners" may be understood to refer to His exaltation "higher than the heavens." The Greek phrase translated "separate" is a perfect passive participle, which would indicate that the separation was not so much something done *by* Jesus as something done *to* Him, and that it occurred at some specific point in the past with results continuing into the present.

that of spatial location. The anthropomorphisms (expressions which describe God in human terms, e.g., the right "hand" of God) in these passages are not intended to mean that Jesus is sitting at a specific location, but that He possesses all power, majesty and authority.[12]

The "heavenly flesh" teaching claims that Jesus had a "heavenly" body which was made higher than the heavens *before* He came to this earth. Hebrews 7:26 disproves this. The word translated "made" (*genomenos*) is an aorist participle which means "becoming," and is correctly translated by the NKJV as "has become higher than the heavens." The high priesthood has to do with Jesus' human nature. His human nature did not preexist the Incarnation "higher than the heavens." It became higher than the heavens only in His exaltation which followed His resurrection.

> "That the Gentiles should be fellowheirs, and of
> the same body, and partakers of his promise in
> Christ by the gospel" (Ephesians 3:6).

"Gentiles engrafted into the same heavenly body with Jews in Christ."

Ephesians 3:6 has nothing to do with the biological nature of the believer's body or of Christ's body. The "body" in view is the church (Ephesians 3:21). This is simply metaphorical language comparing the church to the human body. Paul frequently uses such language. (See I Corinthians 12:12-27; Ephesians 1:23.)

> "And they said, Is not this Jesus, the son of
> Joseph, whose father and mother we know? how
> is it then that he saith, I came down from
> heaven?" (John 6:42).

---

[12] See Bernard Ramm, *Protestant Biblical Hermeneutics* (Grand Rapids, MI: Baker Book House, 1970), 100-101.

> "Is this not the son of Joseph and Mary? No, this is not the son of Joseph and Mary. This is the Son of God."

Here the "heavenly flesh" teaching denies the clear truth of Scripture that Mary was the mother of Jesus. The prophet Isaiah declared, "Therefore the Lord himself shall give you a sign; Behold, a virgin shall conceive, and bear a son, and shall call his name Immanuel" (Isaiah 7:14). Matthew pointed out that this was fulfilled in the conception of Jesus in Mary's womb: "Now all this was done, that it might be fulfilled which was spoken of the Lord by the prophet, saying, Behold, a virgin shall be with child, and shall bring forth a son, and they shall call his name Emmanuel, which being interpreted is, God with us" (Matthew 1:22-23). Mary had *conceived* (Matthew 1:20). Jesus was her "firstborn son" (Matthew 1:25). Contrary to the "heavenly flesh" teaching, Jesus *was* the son of Mary. Acts 1:14 declares plainly that Mary was "the mother of Jesus." The "heavenly flesh" teaching requires that Mary did not conceive in her womb; the "heavenly flesh" was supposedly just deposited in her womb by God. But the consistent teaching of Scripture is that she conceived (Luke 1:31). This requires that she supplied the human egg from which Jesus' humanity was derived.

> "And Simon Peter answered and said, Thou art the Christ, the Son of the living God. ... And I say also unto thee, That thou art Peter, and upon this rock I will build my church; and the gates of hell shall not prevail against it" (Matthew 16:16, 18).

> "This revelation, that He is the heavenly man, the Son of the Living God and not related in any way to the earthy, first Adam is the ROCK of revelation upon which Jesus said He would build a church, His church. The gates of hell may not prevail against it. God bless you."

This interpretation of Matthew 16:16-18 is wide of the mark. The rock upon which the church is built is the confession that Jesus is the Messiah (Christ), the Son of the living God. There is simply nothing in these verses about Jesus being the "heavenly man" unrelated in any way to the first Adam.

> "For no man ever yet hated his own flesh; but nourisheth and cherisheth it, even as the Lord the church: For we are members of his body, of his flesh, and of his bones. For this cause shall a man leave his father and mother, and shall be joined unto his wife, and they two shall be one flesh. This is a great mystery: but I speak concerning Christ and the church" (Ephesians 5:29-32).

---

"The Lord nourisheth and cherisheth the Church, which is His body. We are members of His body, of His flesh and of His bones. The mystery of two becoming one flesh in marriage pertains to Christ and His saints becoming one flesh in the new birth."

---

We have discussed these verses above. They have nothing to do with Christ having "heavenly flesh" or with believers having "heavenly flesh." In this metaphorical language, the intimate relationship between Christ and the church is compared to the intimate relationship between and husband and wife. There is no hint of any biological change in the believer's body when he is born again. Just as a husband and wife become "one flesh" in sexual union without effecting any change in the physical body of either of them, so believers are members of Christ's flesh and bones without effecting any biological change in their human body. The language is figurative, not literal.

> "In whom also ye are circumcised with the circumcision made without hands, in putting off

the body of the sins of the flesh by the circumcision of Christ" (Colossians 2:11).

---

"Baptism is the putting-off of the (Adamic) body of the sins of the (Adamic, earthy) flesh."

---

The "body of the sins of the flesh" is not the physical, human body. It is a reference to "the old nature, which is corrupt in its unregenerate state of rebellion against God."[13] There is absolutely no biological difference between the human body before baptism and after baptism. This is a legal declaration of what occurs at the new birth: the believer is no longer a slave to sin; the righteousness of Jesus Christ is imputed to his account. (See Romans 6:22; II Corinthians 5:21.) This does not mean that the believer no longer struggles with the "flesh," or the sin principle. Long after he was born again, Paul wrote, "... sin ... dwelleth in me. For I know that in me (that is, in my flesh,) dwelleth no good thing ..." (Romans 7:17-18). He also declared that believers are "waiting for the adoption, to wit, the redemption of our body" (Romans 8:23). This clearly means that the human body is not yet redeemed.

> "For as many of you as have been baptized into Christ have put on Christ" (Galatians 3:27).

---

"Put off the earthy man, put on the heavenly man, Christ."

---

The meaning of this verse has been discussed above. It has nothing to do with putting on "heavenly flesh."

> "Knowing this, that our old man is crucified with him, that the body of sin might be destroyed, that henceforth we should not serve sin" (Romans 6:6).

---

[13] Charles C. Ryrie, *The Ryrie Study Bible*, King James Version (Chicago, IL: Moody Press, 1978), 1693.

> "Our old (Adamic, earthy, fleshly) man is crucified with Him that the (earthy) body of sin might be destroyed."

See the discussion under Colossians 2:11 above. The body of sin is not the physical body. It is not our physical body that is crucified with Christ. The "old man" is a reference to the sin nature or sin principle which dwells in every man as a consequence of Adam's sin. (See Romans 5:12; Ephesians 4:22; Colossians 3:9.) It is not necessary for believers to experience physical crucifixion as Jesus did; His death was on our behalf. What is necessary is for the believer to be identified with Jesus in His crucifixion or death. As Paul has just pointed out, this occurs at water baptism (Romans 6:3-4.) Thus baptism, when submitted to in faith, is much more than a mere public profession of one's desire to follow Christ. It actually accomplishes the crucifixion or death of the sin nature, or, in other words, it does away with the "body of sin." This does not mean the believer no longer has the sin nature indwelling him (I John 1:8) or that he can no longer be tempted, for death does not mean extinction. It means separation. Paul's point is that when we are identified with Jesus Christ in His death, the ruling power of sin over us is broken, so that "we should no longer be slaves to sin." The human body without the human spirit is dead (James 1:26), but the human body is not extinct simply because of its separation from the human spirit. It still exists and can be acted upon, although it cannot act. In a similar way, the sin nature, the "body of sin," is not extinct because it is dead. And although it is incapable of acting any longer in such a way as to dominate the believer's life, it can be acted upon by the believer who chooses to yield his members as instruments of unrighteousness unto sin (Romans 6:12-13). It may seem strange at first to think that anyone who is free from domination by the sin nature would yield to sin, but this is precisely what Adam and Eve did in the Garden of Eden. Temptation to sin does not arise from the sin nature, but from the power of choice inherent in being human. Certainly the sin nature enhances temptation and tilts a person more decidedly

47

toward sin, but a person can be tempted on the basis of the power of choice alone. Jesus was tempted, and He certainly did not possess a sin nature. (See Hebrews 4:15.)

One primary difference between the unbeliever and the believer who has been united with Jesus Christ in His death, burial, and resurrection is that the unbeliever is a slave to sin; he has no power to break free from it. (See Romans 6:17-20.) The believer has been set free from sin's controlling power; he has the ability, by the power of the Holy Spirit, to resist temptation. (See Romans 6:12-14, 18.) As Paul puts it, "He who has died has been freed from sin." Identification with Jesus Christ in His death frees the believer from sin's control. It does not give him a new body made of "heavenly flesh."

> "And that ye put on the new man, which after God
> is created in righteousness and true holiness"
> (Ephesians 4:24).

---

"The new man which we have put of [sic] is created in true *righteousness* and *holiness* after God's image."

---

I'm sure the notes mean "the new man which we have put *on.*" Here is seen an inconsistency in the "heavenly flesh" teaching. On the one hand, it teaches that the physical body we had previous to being born again is put off and the new "heavenly flesh" is put on in water baptism. (See "heavenly flesh" teaching on Colossians 2:11 above.) But then it appeals to Ephesians 4:24 which encourages believers to "put on the new man." This can only mean they had not yet done this, even though they were baptized and were thus saints (Ephesians 1:1). The putting on of the new man has nothing to do with "heavenly flesh." The context of Ephesians 4:24 reveals that it has to do with putting away lying, handling anger correctly, giving no place to the devil, stopping stealing, speaking gracious words, refusing to grieve the Holy Spirit, putting away bitterness, wrath, anger, clamor, evil speaking, malice, and being kind, tenderhearted and forgiving (Ephesians 4:25-32).

> "That ye put off concerning the former conversation the old man, which is corrupt according to the deceitful lusts" (Ephesians 4:22).

> "The old, Adamic (earthy, fleshly) man is *'corrupt.'* "

All of the comments immediately above on Ephesians 4:24 apply to this verse. The "old man" is not the physical body of believers before the new birth. The Ephesians were already saints (Ephesians 1:1), but they still needed to put off the "old man." Thus, they had not put him off at baptism, contrary to the "heavenly flesh" teaching. In this context, the "old man" has to do with wrong thinking (Ephesians 4:23.)

> "And when the king came in to see the guests, he saw there a man which had not on a wedding garment: And he saith unto him, Friend, how camest thou in hither not having a wedding garment? And he was speechless" (Matthew 22:11-12). [The notes refer to the entire parable found in Matthew 22:1-14. For the sake of brevity, I have included only the pertinent verses.]

> "Parable of the required outer clothing to be present at the marriage feast."

This parable has nothing to do with "heavenly flesh." The wedding garment was a robe supplied to the guests by the king's servants, since all the guests came hurriedly, directly from the highways, without opportunity to get suitably clothed. This means a person must not only respond externally to the invitation to come to the Lord, but he must also appropriate all that God the king provides in salvation. The "heavenly flesh" teaching reads into the parable something that is not there. The reference in the parable is to a garment of cloth, not to a new physical body.

> "That in the dispensation of the fulness of times he might gather together in one all things in Christ, both which are in heaven, and which are on earth; even in him" (Ephesians 1:10).

| "The mystery of His will is to gather us into His heavenly body." |
| --- |

There is no reference here to a "heavenly body." This verse means that in the end, everything in heaven and on earth will be brought under the authority of Christ. This is something that will occur in the "dispensation of the fulness of times." It has not yet happened, contrary to the teaching of the "heavenly flesh" doctrine.

> "For I delight in the law of God after the inward man" (Romans 7:22).

| "The new 'inward' man delights in the law of God, unlike the old, corrupt, Adamic man." |
| --- |

At the same time that Paul delighted in the law of God after the inward man, he saw another law in his "members, warring against the law of [his] mind, and bringing [him] into captivity to the law of sin which [was] in [his] members" (Romans 7:23). He had both of these experiences simultaneously. He did not have "heavenly flesh" which freed him from temptation. Contextually, the "inward man" is the mind (Romans 6:23). As far as his mind was concerned, Paul would have been delighted to have been able to conform perfectly to the Law of Moses.

> "For the bread of God is he which cometh down from heaven, and giveth life unto the world" (John 6:33).

50

"For I came down from heaven, not to do mine own will, but the will of him that sent me" (John 6:38).

"This is the bread which cometh down from heaven, that a man may eat thereof, and not die. I am the living bread which came down from heaven: if any man eat of this bread, he shall live for ever: and the bread that I will give is my flesh, which I will give for the life of the world" (John 6:50-51).

"This is that bread which came down from heaven: not as your fathers did eat manna, and are dead: he that eateth of this bread shall live for ever" (John 6:58).

> "The heavenly man Christ is come down from heaven unlike the earthy, Adamic man formed from the dust of the earth."

The "heavenly flesh" teaching on this section of Scripture is not far removed from the doctrine of transubstantiation, which says that in the Lord's Supper, the bread is literally transformed into the flesh of Christ, and the fruit of the vine literally becomes the blood of Christ. The "heavenly flesh" teaching says that the flesh of Jesus came down from heaven. Actually, in this entire passage (John 6:32-58), Jesus is using figurative language to point out that just as the ancient Israelites survived by eating manna (John 6:31), people today must believe the words of Jesus (John 6:63-64). To make it clear that He was not saying that people must literally eat His flesh and drink His blood (John 6:56), Jesus said, "It is the spirit that quickeneth; the flesh profiteth nothing: the words that I speak unto you, they are spirit, and they are life" (John 6:63). It is clear that His disciples understood that Jesus was talking about His words, not His flesh (John 6:68). If there were such a thing as "heavenly flesh," it would certainly be profitable. But Jesus said, "The flesh profiteth nothing." The only flesh He mentioned in the entire passage was *His* flesh. Thus He meant that eating His physical flesh would be of no benefit; only the Spirit gives life, and He gives life to those who hear and believe Jesus' words.

If Jesus' body was "heavenly flesh" which came down from heaven, He was not the seed of the woman, He was not the seed of Abraham, He was not the fruit of David's body (Psalm 132:11; Acts 2:30), Mary did not conceive, and she was not His mother. This is contrary to all the Bible teaches on these subjects.

> "For we being many are one bread, and one body: for we are all partakers of that one bread" (I Corinthians 10:17).

> "We are now one body in the new, heavenly man."

Again, this is figurative language. Believers are no more one literal body made up of "heavenly flesh" than they are a loaf of bread! This is simply a reference to the believers' identification with Christ in the Lord's Supper in the same way ancient Israel identified with the sacrifices they offered (I Corinthians 10:18).

> "Nevertheless death reigned from Adam to Moses, even over them that had not sinned after the similitude of Adam's transgression, who is the figure of him that was to come" (Romans 5:14).

> "The earthy man Adam was created in the figure of the heavenly man Christ that was to come."

The word "figure" is translated from the Greek *typos*, which means "type." It has nothing to do with the physical body of Adam. In some sense, Adam was a type of "Him who was to come." This passage indicates that the relationship between Adam and Christ is more one of contrast, rather than of comparison. The similarity between the two has to do with the fact that each had a universal impact on mankind, Adam for evil and Christ for good. There is nothing here about Adam's body or Christ's body.

> "For if by one man's offence death reigned by one; much more they which receive abundance of grace and of the gift of righteousness shall reign in life by one, Jesus Christ.) Therefore as by the offence of one judgment came upon all men to condemnation; even so by the righteousness of one the free gift came upon all men unto justification of life. For as by one man's disobedience many were made sinners, so by the obedience of one shall many be made righteous. Moreover the law entered, that the offence might abound. But where sin abounded, grace did much more abound: That as sin hath reigned unto death, even so might grace reign through righteousness unto eternal life by Jesus Christ our Lord" (Romans 5:17-21).

"For those in the earthy Adam, death reigns; for those in Christ, the Second Adam, life reigns."

This statement is close to the truth, but the insertion of the word "earthy" suggests that Paul's emphasis is on the physical body versus "heavenly flesh." This is not true.

Romans 5:17 means that as a result of Adam's sin, death (spiritual separation from God) reigned universally. But Paul does not say that as a consequence of Christ's work on the cross life (spiritual fellowship with God) now reigns universally. Instead, he says that those who will "reign in life" are those who "*receive* abundance of grace and of the gift of righteousness." The way spiritual life is received is by faith in Jesus Christ. (See John 1:12; Romans 3:22, 26, 30; 4:11-12, 16, 24; 5:1-2.)

Paul uses the phrase "much more" to demonstrate the superiority of Christ's work over Adam's sin. (See also Romans 5:15, 20.) The grace (free gift) received by believers is *abundant*; it is more than necessary to achieve the desired result. (See Romans 3:25.)

Paul identifies righteousness (right standing with God) as a free gift extended to those who "receive abundance of grace." Throughout this letter, he emphasizes the fact that favor with God is not earned by one's performance, but received as a free gift by those who rely exclusively on Jesus Christ for salvation.

Romans 5:17 concludes the parenthetical statement beginning in verse 13, and in Romans 5:18 Paul contrasts the universal impact of Adam's sin directly with the universal impact of "one Man's righteous act." The NKJV translation of this verse is helpful: "Therefore, as through one man's offense judgment came to all men, resulting in condemnation, even so through one Man's righteous act the free gift came to all men, resulting in justification of life." The sin of Adam resulted in all men being condemned, for all men participated with him in his sin, either by representation or by being present in his loins. But though the righteous act of Jesus Christ results in all men being *potentially* justified, men must *receive* the free gift by faith in order to actually be justified. The reason for this difference is that all men were *not* participants in the atonement in the same way all men were participants in Adam's sin. Although Jesus stood in complete solidarity with the human race by virtue of his genuine humanity, he was spared the spiritual separation from God resulting from Adam's sin by the miracle of the virgin birth. Since God was His Father, He was not born in a state of spiritual separation from God. Thus Jesus could *represent* us on the cross, but we were not physically present in His righteous deed as we were in Adam's sin. As a result, we participate in Adam's sin by nature, but not in Christ's atonement. In order to participate in the results of Christ's atonement, we must completely and exclusively trust in and rely upon the efficacy of the blood of Jesus for our salvation. (See Romans 3:25.) The free gift does come to all men, but it is still necessary for all men to receive it.

Romans 5:19 means that as a result of Adam's sin, the many (the entire human race) became sinners. The spiritual separation from God resulting from Adam's sin assured that each human being would commit his own personal sins. It is important to note from Paul's argument that the human race did not initially become sinners on the basis of their individual sins; they became sinners on the basis of one man's sin. By contrast, the many (potentially the entire human race, but specifically those who receive the gift, Romans 5:17), will be returned to right standing with God not on the basis of their personal righteous performance, but on the basis of "one Man's obedience." This is in perfect harmony with Paul's emphasis throughout this letter that men gain right standing with God not on the basis of their righteous deeds, but on the basis of the righteousness of Jesus Christ. If we can believe that we experience spiritual separation from God as a consequence, not of specific sins we have committed, but of what Adam did, we should also be able to believe that we experience spiritual reconciliation with God not on the basis of our own righteous works, but on the basis of the work of Jesus Christ. This can remove forever the fear that naturally accompanies the belief that our right standing with God depends upon our own performance. Those who are secure in their right standing with God find it much easier to conform to right behavior than those who live constantly in the fear that they must "get good to get God." (See Romans 7:5-11.)

Romans 5:10 is one of the places where Paul explains the purpose of the Law of Moses. Though many purposes can be deduced from Scripture, Paul here points out one of them: The Law of Moses was given to emphasize sin. Grammatically, the phrase "that the offense might abound" can be a purpose clause or a result clause. In other words, it can refer to the purpose for which the Law was given or the result of the Law being given. Regardless of which meaning we choose, the fact is that the Law of Moses aroused sinful passions. (See Romans 7:5-11.) Men were already sinners, but the Law aggravated the sin problem. This was intentional on God's part; He intended to demonstrate without question the universal sinfulness of man, so that all men would recognize their need of a Savior. (See Galatians 3:19-25.) But although the Law of Moses made it very clear that men were sinners, the grace of God surpassed the sinfulness of men in providing salvation.

Romans 5:21 points out that just as sin had universally condemned all men to spiritual separation from God (death), so grace provides universal right standing with God which will result in eternal life for all those who receive it. This eternal life is through Jesus Christ our Lord. Thus concludes Paul's discussion of the contrast between Adam and Jesus, a subject he takes up in other letters as well. (See I Corinthians 15:21-22, 45-49.)

There is nothing in this passage to support the "heavenly flesh" teaching.

> "And you, that were sometime alienated and enemies in your mind by wicked works, yet now hath he reconciled in the body of his flesh through death, to present you holy and unblameable and unreproveable in his sight" (Colossians 1:21-22).

"We are reconciled to God by reason of the (sinless, heavenly) body of His flesh."

This comment inserts words into the Scriptural text which are simply not there. There is not one place in Scripture where the flesh of Jesus is said to be "heavenly flesh." We are reconciled in the body of His flesh because His body was just like ours and could thus be a substitute for us. If Jesus had "heavenly flesh," His death could not be a substitute for us.

> "And the angel answered and said unto her, The Holy Ghost shall come upon thee, and the power of the Highest shall overshadow thee: therefore also that holy thing which shall be born of thee shall be called the Son of God" (Luke 1:35).

> "The Angel declared the Second Adam to be 'a holy thing,' 'the Son of God,' begotten by the overshadowing of the Holy Ghost and the power of the Highest (not of the earth, earthy, like Adam)."

It is true that the angel told Mary her Son would be a "holy thing." But this does not mean Jesus would have "heavenly flesh." Instead, he said she would "conceive" (Luke 1:30), which required that she supply the egg for the child. He also said that Jesus would be given "the throne of his father David" (Luke 1:32). David was Jesus' father because Jesus was the fruit of David's loins (Psalm 132:11; Acts 2:30). The angel also said that Jesus would be born of Mary (Luke 1:35). Mary conceived just as did her cousin Elizabeth (Luke 1:36). The angel also told Joseph that Mary had conceived (Matthew 1:20).

There is nothing in Luke 1:35 to suggest that Jesus' humanity was "heavenly." Mary was no surrogate mother. The baby was conceived in her womb (Luke 2:21).

> "Verily I say unto you, Among them that are born
> of women there hath not risen a greater than John
> the Baptist: notwithstanding he that is least in the
> kingdom of heaven is greater than he" (Matthew
> 11:11).

> "All who are born again into the body of Christ are greater than the greatest who is still in the Adamic man."

This verse has nothing to do with the nature of John's physical body or the nature of a believer's body. All that this means is that under the Old Covenant, no one was greater than John, but that under the New Covenant, those who are born again enjoy a position of greater intimacy with God.

57

"Being born again, not of corruptible seed, but of incorruptible, by the word of God, which liveth and abideth for ever" (I Peter 1:23).

> "We are born first into the corruptible, earthy, Adamic man, but the second time, we are born of incorruptible seed, by the word of God."

This statement is true, so far as it goes. But the implication is that when we are born again, we receive an incorruptible body. This is not true. In this examination of the "heavenly flesh" teaching, we have seen that the abundant testimony of Scripture is that there is no biological change in the believer's body when he is born again. There will be no change in his body until the body is redeemed at the appearing of Jesus (Romans 8:23; I John 3:2; Colossians 3:4; Philippians 3:20-21; I Corinthians 15:51-54.)

# Heavenly Flesh: A Response

In this chapter I respond to what I perceive to be the key points of the heavenly flesh teaching as found in *Bible Writers' Theology*.[14] The following format is used: First, direct quotes from the book are enclosed in a box. The numbers following the quotes are the page numbers on which the quotes are found. Putting the page numbers with the quotes avoids the unnecessary multiplication of footnotes. Second, my comments follow the quotes. Unless otherwise indicated, all quotes from Scripture in my comments will be from the New King James Version. The abbreviation *BWT* stands for *Bible Writers' Theology*.

> "... according to the human reasoning of some, Jesus is an ordinary man of earthly flesh and blood with His own independent human spirit. ... the oneness of God would actually be two persons: the Father, who has an independent personality, and Christ, with His own independent personality" (120).
>
> "The Bible says, 'God was manifested in the flesh.' It does not say God was manifested in an independent man" (121).

This is not the view of Oneness Pentecostalism. Jesus' human spirit is not "independent." Oneness Pentecostalism does not embrace Nestorianism. Jesus is a genuine, authentic human being in whom the fullness of the Godhead (*theotetos*, "divine nature") dwells. The divine nature is manifest in His body, in His soul, in His spirit, in all that makes Him a human being. In the words of I Timothy 3:16, God is manifest in every aspect of Jesus' human existence. Thus, although Jesus is a genuine human being, He is not "independent" in any way from God. He is God

---

[14] Teklemariam Gezahagne, *Bible Writers' Theology* (n.p.: Ozark Mountain Press, 1999).

59

manifest in a genuine human being. The *BWT* views human existence in a fragmented way that is foreign to Hebrew thought and more in keeping with Greek philosophy.

> "The truth and very foundation of the church, as well as our salvation, is that Christ is the Son of the living God by nature. **All that will receive everlasting life must have this same revelation**" (121; emphasis in original).

In the context of this chapter, this seems to mean that one must agree with the *BWT* view of Jesus' humanity to be saved. It is not enough to believe what the Bible says and to confess what Scripture confesses; one must have a "revelation" that explains away the clear teaching of Scripture.

> "God was manifested in the flesh and blood of Himself. God, like man, has two aspects: inner and outer nature. The inner aspect is God the Father, and the outer aspect is the Son, Christ Jesus, the flesh and blood of God, the express image of His person" (122).

None of the Scriptures given to prove this point have anything to say about this concept. To say that "God was manifested in the flesh and blood of Himself" renders the Incarnation meaningless. It violates everything Scripture says about the Messiah being the descendent of Adam, of Eve, of Abraham, and of David. God is a Spirit, and a Spirit does not have flesh. (See John 4:24; Luke 24:39.)

> "He said, 'In the beginning was the Word, and the Word was with God and God (Himself) was the Word.' (See Greek Bible)" (123).

This is not what John 1:1 says. It is a mistranslation. The last phrase of the verse, *kai theos ēn ho logos,* cannot be translated "and God (Himself) was the Word." This is why no legitimate translation renders the phrase this way. The subject of this phrase, identified by the article and in the nominative case, is *logos,* "word." *Theos* does not have the definite article, and it is a predicate nominative. Grammatically, it attributes quality to the subject. The point is, the Word is divine. To be divine is to be God.

> "No man can prove the biological relationship of Christ with Mary's flesh and blood" (123).

If the Bible is accepted as authoritative, and if the words are taken to mean what they say, the biological relationship of Christ with Mary's flesh and blood certainly can be proven.

> Therefore the Lord Himself will give you a sign:
> Behold, the virgin shall conceive and bear a Son,
> and shall call His name Immanuel (Isaiah 7:14;
> see Matthew 1:23).

The virgin herself would conceive. In the case of the "heavenly flesh" teaching, Mary did not conceive, for she contributed nothing to the birth of Jesus. She was merely an incubator or surrogate mother who provided a womb for a baby conceived without any contribution on her part. Throughout the Old Testament the word most commonly translated "conceive" (*harah*) is used in reference to women who conceived children. Isaiah 7:14 proves the biological relationship between Christ and Mary.

> ...do not be afraid to take to you Mary your wife,
> for that which is conceived in her is of the Holy
> Spirit (Matthew 1:20).

The word translated "conceived" (*gennēthen,* aorist passive participle, nominative neuter singular of *gennaō* [I bear, I give birth to]) is the causal form of *ginōmai* (I become) which, when used of the father, means "to beget, to engender" and when used of the mother, means "to bring forth." The word is used to indicate precisely what the *BWT* denies: the biological relationship between a parent and an offspring. The idea of a surrogate mother (*BWT*, 174) was completely foreign to the world of the Bible.

> And Jacob begot Joseph the husband of Mary, of whom was born Jesus who is called Christ (Matthew 1:16).

Matthew is careful here to point out that there is no biological relationship between Joseph and Jesus, but that there is a biological relationship between Mary and Jesus. "Of whom" (literally, "out of whom" [*ex hēs*]) indicates that Jesus was of Mary. *Hēs* is the feminine singular relative pronoun in the genitive case, referring to Mary. The preposition *ex* ("out of") indicates that Jesus biologically (*egennēthē*) came from Mary.

> And behold, you will conceive in your womb and bring forth a Son, and shall call His name JESUS (Luke 1:31).

The phrase *syllēmpsē en gastri* indicates the biological relationship between Mary and Jesus. *Syllēmpsē*, a future middle deponent indicative second person singular form of *syllambanō*, means "to conceive." Because of its connection with the woman's part in conception, the word was used by Thucydides (5th century B.C.) to mean "to contribute towards a thing."

The conception of Jesus occurred *en gastri*, or "in the womb." Again, the idea of a surrogate mother was completely foreign to biblical thought, and the idea here is that Mary was biologically connected to Jesus in the same what the John was biologically connected to Elizabeth (see Luke 1:36). How could it be that Mary could actually conceive without a human male sperm? "For with God nothing will be impossible" (Luke 1:37). If the "heavenly flesh" teaching is true, no one during the past 2,000 years could have understood it; the understanding of it would have awaited the development of surrogate motherhood.

And it happened, when Elizabeth heard the greeting of Mary, that the babe leaped in her womb; and Elizabeth was filled with the Holy Spirit. Then she spoke out with a loud voice and said, 'Blessed are you among women, and blessed is the fruit of your womb! But why is this granted to me, that the mother of my Lord should come to me? (Luke 1:41-43).

Elizabeth spoke by the influence of the Holy Spirit. She identified the child in Mary's womb as the *karpos* (fruit) of her womb. In every case that *karpos* is used in the New Testament, a genetic relationship is in view, whether it is natural fruit, spiritual fruit, or human conception.

By the influence of the Holy Spirit, Elizabeth calls Mary "the mother of my Lord."

But when the fullness of the time had come, God sent forth His Son, made of a woman, made under the law (Galatians 4:4).

The *BWT* misinterprets this verse:

Some use Galatians 4:4 to prove that Jesus took part of His nature from God the Father, and part of His nature from Mary. They indicate that the scripture here clearly states that the **Son was 'made' of a woman;** 'made' indicating part of the woman, Mary was taken to make the flesh of Jesus. Or the Son of God biologically became Son of Mary. They think the word that became flesh (Jesus) was changed into Mary's nature. …

The same word that is used to validate the claim that Jesus was 'made' of the flesh of earthly Mary, is used again in the same scripture. It says that the Son was 'made' under the law. If the argument is true that the Son was 'made' of a part

63

of the woman, we could also say that the Son was 'made' out of a part of the law. Can we say part of Mary's flesh plus part of the law is equal Christ? No one would dare say that the Son (the flesh) was actually made out of a part of the law. Why then are there those who say that the Son was made out of part of the woman, and use this scripture as proof of their claim? ...

. . . The Greek word that is used in both instances in Galatians 4:4 is 'ginomai'. According to Strong's Exhaustive Concordance of the Bible, 'ginomai' means 'to cause to be, to become (come into being)', and notes it is used with 'great latitude'. ...

Other possible definitions of 'ginomai' are: 'be fulfilled', 'be kept', 'be ordained', and 'be found'. None of these possible definitions imply that a part of Mary was used in the making of the flesh. 'Ginomai' is not used to refer to the natural offspring, or the biological seed . . . (182-183).

The *BWT* misrepresents the belief of those who hold to the genuineness of the Incarnation. We do not say that Jesus took "part" of His nature from God the Father, and "part" of His nature from Mary. Instead, Jesus received His divine nature from God and His human nature from Mary. Jesus is not "half God" and "half human." He is a full and complete human being in whom the fullness of the divine nature dwells.

Secondly, the *BWT* misunderstands the Greek text of Galatians 4:4. In the effort to equate "being made of a woman" with "being made under the law," the *BWT* ignores the prepositions and completely misreads the text. Jesus was made *ek gynaikos* (out of a woman), He was not made *ek nomou* (out of the law); He was made *hypo nomon* (under the law). To say that Jesus was made "out of" a woman indicates His biological relationship with Mary. To say that Jesus was made "under" the law indicates that the Law of Moses was in effect when Jesus was born.

The word translated "made" (*genomenon*) is an aorist middle deponent participle in the accusative case, masculine gender, and singular in number. The word comes from *ginomai* (I become). Grammatically, Galatians 4:4 declares that the Son "came to be out of a woman," indicating Jesus' biological connection to Mary.

The *BWT* says "'ginomai' is not used to refer to the natural offspring, or the biological seed." This is, however, precisely how the word is used here and in Romans 1:3: "concerning His Son Jesus Christ our Lord, which was made of the seed of David according to the flesh." This is a precise statement concerning the biological connection of Jesus with David. *Genomenou* is the genitive masculine singular form of the aorist middle deponent participle from *ginomai*. Jesus was made *ek spermatos* (out of the seed) of David *kata sarka* (according to the flesh). That is, so far as the flesh of Jesus is concerned, it was made out of the seed of David. Mary was, of course, the seed, or a descendent, of David.

---

"Many so-called Christians ... are confused about the origin of Christ's flesh. ... anyone that does not believe in the Incarnation of the Father in the Son is both a liar and antichrist. ... Whoever denies the inseparable oneness of His Godhead also denies the express image of God's person, the Father manifested in the flesh; and such a man is indeed antichrist" (125-126).

---

In the context of the *BWT*, this seems to question the genuineness of the Christianity of anyone who does not agree with the "heavenly flesh" error. If we are "confused about the origin of Christ's flesh" (i.e., if we believe He received His human nature from Mary), we are "so-called Christians." Indeed, we are "antichrist."

---

"God will not mingle His holy, divine nature with sinful humanity" (129).

---

Oneness Pentecostism does not teach that God did this. The sin nature is not inherent to human nature. The sin nature is actually a blemish on human nature. Neither Adam nor Eve had the sin nature before they sinned, yet they were fully human. Jesus was spared the sin nature by the miracle of the virgin conception. How could this be? "For with God nothing will be impossible" (Luke 1:37). The *BWT* asserts that there is indeed something impossible with God, and that is that the Messiah could be biologically related to the virgin Mary and yet be without sin.

> "The Son of God grew up out of a dry gound: the virgin womb" (130).

The *BWT* repeatedly interprets the "dry ground" of Isaiah 53:2 as a reference to the virgin womb. There is nothing in the context to indicate that this connection is correct. Instead, "Isaiah uses the image of a plant shallowly rooted in dry ground to emphasize the apparent insignificance of the Lord's special suffering servant."[15] The context in which this metaphor is found indicates that this is the correct meaning. Isaiah did not say that the Messiah *is* a root out of dry ground. He said the Messiah would "grow up ... *as* a root out of dry ground." The word "as' indicates this is a metaphor, not to be taken literally.

> "Christ never gave recognition to Mary as being His mother. Instead, He asked, 'Who is my mother?' To Mary He said, 'Woman, what have I to do with thee?' In the days of His flesh, Jesus never, called Mary 'My mother'" (130).

Certainly Jesus gave recognition to Mary as being His mother. When Jesus lingered in the temple at the age of twelve, Joseph and "His mother" (Luke 2:43) returned to find Him sitting in the midst of the teachers. "So when they saw Him, they were

---

[15] Leland Ryken, et al., *Dictionary of Biblical Imagery* (Downers Grove, IL: InterVarsity Press, 1998), 741.

amazed; and His mother said to him, 'Son, why have You done this to us? ... Then He went down with them and came to Nazareth, and was subject to them, but His mother kept all these things in her heart" (Luke 2:48, 51). Jesus would not have returned home with Mary unless He had recognized her as His mother.

> When Jesus therefore saw His mother, and the disciple whom He loved standing by, He said to His mother, "Woman, behold your son!" (John 19:26).

Because the precise words "my mother" are not recorded in the gospels as being spoken by Jesus in recognition of Mary as His mother, the *BWT* argues from silence that Mary was not His mother. It is never appropriate to argue from silence, but the *BWT* uses this approach to disregard at least twenty-three references in the inspired Scripture to Mary as the mother of Jesus. These twenty-three references exclude other references to Mary as Jesus' mother that could have been simply someone's opinion. These references are inspired of the Holy Spirit. To disregard them is to deny the inerrancy of Scripture.[16]

To say "Christ never gave recognition to Mary as being His mother" is wrong. When Jesus said to the disciple He loved, "Behold thy mother," He was recognizing His responsibility to His mother as her eldest Son and assigning that responsibility to one whom He loved, apparently in view of the fact that His younger brothers were not at that time people of faith.

To say that Jesus never called Mary His mother is to assume omniscience as to all of the words Jesus spoke while He was on this earth from the time He began to talk until His resurrection, even though we have record of only a few months of His life. What is more significant is to point out that Jesus never said, "Mary is not my mother." When He said, "Who is my mother,

---

[16] See Matthew 1:18; 2:11, 13-14, 20-21; 12:46; Mark 3:31; Luke 1:43; 2:33-34, 43, 48, 51; 8:19; John 2:1, 3, 5, 12; 19:25-27; Acts 1:14.

and who are my brothers?", Jesus was not denying that Mary was His mother or that He had brothers. He was, instead, reaching out to include as members of His larger family all who are people of faith.

When Jesus said to Mary, "Woman, what does your concern have to do with Me? My hour has not yet come" (John 2:4), it was no show of disrespect or disowning of His mother. In the first century, to call His mother "woman" was the equivalent of the modern "Ma'am." The NIV offers a dynamically equivalent translation: "Dear woman, why do you involve me? My time has not yet come." (See John 4:21; 8:10; 19:26; 20:15.) The Greek text *Ti emoi kai soi* translates literally "what to me and to you?" The idea is, "How does this concern of yours concern me?" The phrase has nothing to do with the biological relationship between Mary and Jesus.

---

"Some theologians think David's personal confessions are of Jesus" (130).

---

The theologians who think this include Jesus, Peter, Paul, and the writer of Hebrews.[17] The New Testament is rich in references to the Messianic Psalms. The specific psalm referred to in the *BWT*, Psalm 69, includes clear references to the life and experiences of Jesus. Compare Psalm 69:21 with Matthew 27:34, 48 and John 19:28-30. Compare Psalm 69:25 with Acts 1:20. Compare Psalm 69:9 with John 2:17. Compare Psalm 69:22-28 with Romans 11:9-10.

Apparently, the reason the *BWT* wishes to deny the Messianic content of the psalms is to avoid the significance of Psalm 69:8: "I have become a stranger to my brothers, and an alien to my mother's children." The *BWT* reads, "As people suppose they may say Christ had biological brothers and sisters

---

[17] See Daniel L. Segraves, *The Messiah in the Psalms: Discovering Christ in Unexpected Places* (Hazelwood, MO: Word Aflame Press, 2007) and Daniel L. Segraves, *Reading Between the Lines: Discovering Christ in the Old Testament* (Hazelwood, MO: Word Aflame Press, 2008).

...." In denying that Jesus had biological brothers and sisters, the *BWT* adopts the opinion of the Roman Catholic Church and denies the literal statements of Scripture.[18]

> "David could not be the biological father of Christ, for Christ is not from human seed. He was the heavenly Adam" (131).

This statement is in specific opposition to the teaching of Scripture:

> Therefore, being a prophet, and knowing that God had sworn with an oath to him that of the fruit of his body, according to the flesh, He would raise up the Christ to sit on his throne, he, foreseeing this, spoke concerning the resurrection of the Christ, that His soul was not left in Hades, nor did His flesh see corruption (Acts 2:30-31).

In this reference to Psalm 132:11, Peter specifically declares the biological connection between David and Christ. Christ is *ek karpou tēs osphous autou to kata sarka* (out of the fruit of his loins, according to the flesh). To say that Christ is the fruit of David's loins means that He is literally and physically descended from David. This is further indicated in that His descent is "according to the flesh."

Paul agreed with Peter concerning Christ's physical descent from David:

> concerning His Son Jesus Christ our Lord, who was born of the seed of David according to the flesh (Romans 1:3).

A literal and rough translation of this text would be as follows: "concerning the Son of him, the One being made out of the seed of David, according to the flesh."

---

[18] See Matthew 12:46-47; 13:55-56; John 2:12; 7:3, 5, 10; Acts 1:14.

> "'For I came down from heaven, not to do mine own will, but the will of him that sent me' (John 6:38). One will, the Father's only" (132).

The second phrase of this sentence, "not to do mine own will," indicates that Christ had a will distinct from—but not independent of—the will of the Father. This is further indicated in His prayer, "Father, if it is Your will, take this cup away from Me; nevertheless not My will, but Yours, be done" (Luke 22:42 [See also Matthew 26:39]). To deny the genuineness of Christ's human will is Monotheletism. At best, Monotheletism holds to an incomplete Incarnation, fragmenting human nature in a way foreign to biblical thought.

> "If the father begets his son after his likeness, it is true that the law of sin is transmitted to the child, through the combination of the seed and the egg. David also affirms this by saying, 'Behold, I was shapen in iniquity; and in sin did my mother conceive me' (Psalm 51:5)" (134).

The *BWT* several times refers to Psalm 51:5 in an effort to support its view of the impossibility that the Messiah descended biologically from David, even though other Scriptures specifically declare His biological descent. (See Acts 2:30; Romans 1:3.)

Even if it is the point of Psalm 51:5 that "the law of sin is transmitted to the child, through the combination of the seed and the egg"—and that is by no means certain—this does not prohibit Jesus from being biologically descended from David. The virgin conception is a miracle, and when miracles occur natural law is suspended or superseded. Gabriel's explanation as to how Mary could conceive without a husband was, "With God nothing will be impossible" (Luke 1:37). The *BWT* says that it is impossible for the Messiah to be a physical descendent of David without partaking of the sin nature; the Bible says nothing will be impossible with God.

Even though it is true that as a consequence of Adam's sin all humans (except the Messiah) have become sinners, it is doubtful that was David's point in Psalm 51:5. Understood this way, Psalm 51:5 would mean that the very process of conception is sinful and that the shaping of the child in the womb of its mother is an act of iniquity. Nowhere does Scripture suggest that the conception of a child in a marriage relationship is sinful or that the process of the shaping of the child is iniquitous. David himself wrote, "For You formed my inward parts; You covered me in my mother's womb. I will praise you, for I am fearfully and wonderfully made; marvelous are Your works, and that my soul knows very well" (Psalm 139:13-14).

It is more likely that Psalm 51:5 reflects the continuing effect of Judah's sin with Tamar. (See Genesis 38:11-30.) The Law of Moses prohibited anyone from entering into the congregation to the tenth generation after such a sin. (See Deuteronomy 23:2.) David was precisely the tenth generation from the incestuous union of Judah and Tamar. (See I Chronicles 2:3-15: [1] Perez [one of the twins born of incest between Judah and Tamar]; [2] Hezron; [3] Ram; [4] Amminadab; [5] Nahshon; [6] Salma; [7] Boaz; [8] Obed; [9] Jesse; [10] David.) David's confession in Psalm 51:5 is personal: "Behold, *I* was brought forth in iniquity, and in sin *my* mother conceived me." He is not speaking here on behalf of the entire human race, but on his own behalf in a prayer of repentance.

The *BWT* appeals to Job 25:4b several times in an attempt to indicate the impossibility of the sinlessness of Jesus if He is biologically connected to Mary: "Or how can he be pure who is born of a woman?" This neglects the first part of the verse: "How then can man be righteous before God?" Although we should be cautious about using the musings of Job's comforters to establish theology, this verse cannot be used to indicate the impossibility of one who is pure being born of a woman any more than it can be used to indicate the impossibility of a man being righteous before God. A man can be righteous before God by the miracle of justification by faith (see Romans 4:3, 5), and the Messiah can be born of a woman and yet be pure by the miracle of the virgin conception.

The *BWT* also appeals to Job 14:4 in an attempt to indicate the impossibility of the sinlessness of Jesus if He is biologically connected to Mary: "Who can bring a clean thing out of an unclean? No one!" Again, we should be careful about establishing theology from Job's attempt to find the cause of his suffering. But this verse cannot be used to deny the possibility of the sinless Messiah being born of a woman. It may be that no human being can "bring a clean thing out of an unclean," but God specializes in this by the miracle of redemption. "But Peter said, 'Not so, Lord! For I have never eaten anything common or unclean.' And a voice spoke to him again the second time, 'What God has cleansed you must not call common'" (Acts 10:14-15).

> "Genesis 1:27 clearly teaches us that God created the future spiritual Adam in His spiritual image (Tselem) by predestination .... Accordingly in Genesis 2:7, we see God creating the outer man from the dust of the ground in His likeness (Demuth), which is not the same as 'image' in the Hebrew translation. 'Tselem' speaks of the spiritual likeness while 'demuth' speaks of the appearance likeness. 'Demuth' or likeness limits man from the divine nature" (135).

The *BWT* errs at this point and seems to suggest that human beings are not made in the image of God, but that only the "future spiritual Adam" is made "in His spiritual image." An attempt is made to restrict *tselem* to the "spiritual likeness" and to limit this to Jesus and to say that humans are made only in the *demuth* (likeness) of God. This is directly contradicted by Genesis 9:6: "Whoever sheds man's blood, by man his blood shall be shed; For in the image (*tselem*) of God He made man."

*Tselem* is not a reference to spiritual likeness only. The word is used of images of tumors, golden mice, and other false gods. It is used of painted pictures of men. *Demuth* is used in very much the same way. Actually, both words are used in Genesis 1:26 in an apparent poetic device: *betzelmenu kedmutenu* (in our image and in our likeness). *Ke* is a particle of comparison. The words are to be taken as explicating one another, not as presenting two radically different ideas.

The *BWT* is wrong when it says that "'Tselem' speaks of the spiritual likeness while 'demuth' speaks of the appearance likeness." It is also wrong in suggesting that in Genesis 2:7 God creates "the outer man from the dust of the ground in His likeness (Demuth)." The word *demuth* does not appear in Genesis 2:7.

The error of the *BWT* in suggesting that only "the future spiritual Adam" was created in the "spiritual image (Tselem)" of God "by predestination" may be seen in Genesis 1:27: "So God created man in His own image (*tselem*); in the image (*tselem*) of God He created him; male and female He created them." Not only did God create man in His *tselem*; both the male and the female were created in the *tselem* of God.

Another point that should be noted is that throughout Genesis 1:26-27, the Hebrew word translated "man" is *adam* (earthling). It is those who are made of the earth (*haadamah*, Genesis 2:7) that are made in the *tselem* of God.

---

"Romans 8:3 tells us, 'For what the law could not do, in that it was weak through the flesh, God sending his own Son in the likeness of sinful flesh, and for sin, condemned sin in the flesh.' Here the likeness means the form not the actual sinful nature" (136).

---

The *BWT*'s point is not made here, for Paul did not write, "the likeness of flesh," but "the likeness of sinful flesh." If Paul had written, "the likeness of flesh," it would have been a denial of the Incarnation. If he had written, "in sinful flesh," it would have been a denial of Christ's sinlessness. Under the inspiration of the Holy Spirit, the words are precise: they preserve the genuineness of Christ's humanity as well as His sinlessness. Paul wrote that the Son "condemned [judged] sin *in the flesh*."

---

"Biologically, the woman has no seed of herself" (136).

---

And I will put enmity between you and the woman, and between your seed and her seed (Genesis 3:15)

And the dragon was wroth with the woman, and went to make war with the remnant of her seed, which keep the commandments of God, and have the testimony of Jesus Christ (Revelation 12:17).[19]

The Hebrew *zerah* and the Greek *sperma* are used for both men and woman in Scripture to designate their offspring. The *BWT* tries to make a biological point based on modern science that is not in view in Scripture. In the language of the Bible, a woman's descendant is her seed, her offspring, connected biologically with her by means of the egg.

> "Christ was the promised Word, the divine seed, and not the seed of the earthly Adam (I Peter 1:23-25). The Bible calls Him incorruptible seed. Mary's humanity was created from dust through the first Adam, but Christ's humanity is the Word become flesh. ... This shows there is no blood relationship between Mary and Christ. The dry ground is a metaphorical phrase of the unproductive womb of Mary. Christ was not a partaker of Mary's nature or blood" (137).

In these words, it is clear that the *BWT* denies Christ's solidarity with humans. He is not one of us. When the word "flesh" is used of us, it means one thing, but when it is used of Christ, it means something else. Specifically, "the Word became genuine heavenly man in the womb of Mary" (page 137).

The error of the *BWT* on this point may be seen as follows: In I Peter 1:23-25, "word" refers not to Christ but to the gospel message. Although *logos* certainly does refer to Christ in some contexts (e.g., John 1:1, 14; I John 1:1), that does not mean it refers to Christ in every context. Context determines the meaning of words. In this case, *logos* (verse 23) is used as a synonym for *rhema* (verse 25), which is never a reference to Christ. The words have overlapping ranges of meaning, and in this case the overlap is at the point of reference to spoken words. The Hebrew *dabar*, which is translated *rhema* in verse 25 from Isaiah 40:8, makes the text mean, "But the saying of the LORD endures forever."

---

[19] Although the language of Revelation 12:17 is metaphorical, it is based on literal truth.

The *BWT* declares that Christ is "not the seed of the earthly Adam." This is denied by Luke 3:23, 38. The statement "as was supposed" in Luke 3:23 does not negate the entire genealogy of Jesus, making it Jewish tradition, as asserted by the *BWT*. This genealogy differs from the genealogy of Matthew because Matthew presents Jesus' legal claim to the throne through Joseph while Luke presents Jesus' biological claim to the throne through Mary. There is no contradiction between these genealogies. Joseph is the son-in-law of Heli. Mary is not included in this genealogy because it was not customary in Jewish genealogies to list the mother as the final ancestor. The statement "as was supposed" refers only to the lack of a biological connection between Joseph and Jesus, not to the lack of a biological connection between Mary and Jesus or between Jesus and anyone else in the genealogy. If the *BWT* claims were true, Luke's genealogy is at best irrelevant and at worse in error. In either case, it would not belong in the Bible.

According to I Chronicles 1:1, Adam is the ancestor of the entire human race. If Jesus is a human being, He is descended from Adam, as is indicated in Luke's genealogy.

> "The following scriptures give us clear insight concerning the spiritual human nature of Jesus Christ. Still there are those who have not yet seen who the Lord Jesus Christ is …. This question asked by Christ must be answered correctly even today. In order to do so, it requires a revelation from God …. It is necessary to have a scripturally correct explanation of the identity of Christ" (138).

The *BWT* indicates that those who do not agree with its Christology "have not yet seen who the Lord Jesus Christ is." To see who He is "requires a revelation from God." It is "necessary to have a scripturally correct explanation of the identity of Christ."

With these words, the *BWT* dismisses as deficient the understanding of those who believe the inspired Scriptures teach that Jesus is a genuine human being biologically connected to Mary. They do not really know the Lord Jesus Christ. To know Him requires a revelation, apparently in addition to the words of Scripture. This is an appeal to extra-biblical revelation and authority. According to the *BWT*, to understand Christology as it does is not an option, it is "necessary."

> "Tracing the genealogy of Jesus, Luke wrote, 'And Jesus himself began to be about thirty years of age, being (as was supposed) the son of Joseph' (Luke 3:23). Having used the words 'as was supposed', it is clear that to Luke, the long genealogy connecting Christ to Adam, was no more than prevailing Jewish tradition of his day" (139)

According to this view, Luke was *not* tracing the genealogy of Jesus. This view dismisses the entire inspired genealogy as nothing more than "prevailing Jewish tradition." This is difficult to distinguish from the claim that Scripture contains factual errors.

Luke's genealogy is the record of Christ's descent from Adam through David and Mary. The phrase "as was supposed" refers only to the lack of a biological relationship between Joseph and Jesus. The genealogy does not include Mary as the immediate ancestor of Jesus because Jewish custom did not include the mother in a genealogy as the last immediate ancestor. Heli was Joseph's father-in-law. Joseph's father was Jacob. (See Matthew 1:16.) Matthew records Jesus' genealogy through Joseph. Luke records His genealogy through Mary. The two are identical down to David. They differ from David on, with Joseph being descended from David through Solomon (Matthew 1:6) and Mary being descended from David through Nathan (Luke 3:31).

These distinct genealogies are divinely ordained. If Jesus descended from David through Solomon, He would have been disqualified to sit on the throne of David because of the stigma associated with Coniah, also known as Jeconiah. (See Jeremiah 22:28-30; Matthew 1:11.) But in order to qualify to sit on the throne of David, Jesus had to be a descendant of David. (See Acts 2:30; Romans 1:3.) He was a physical descendant of David through His mother Mary. Through his adopted father, Jesus received the legal right to sit on the throne. Through his biological mother, Jesus received the genetic right to sit on the throne. If Jesus is not physically descended from David, He cannot sit on the throne of David.

The first verse of the New Testament makes it clear that Jesus is descended from David: "The book of the genealogy of Jesus Christ, the Son of David, the Son of Abraham" (Matthew 1:1). Matthew 1:16 makes it clear that Jesus was biologically descended from Mary, not Joseph: "And Jacob begot Joseph the

husband of Mary, of whom was born Jesus who is called Christ."
The phrase "of whom was born" (*ex hēs egennēthē*) means that
Jesus was "begotten" or "engendered" "out of" Mary. Although
we commonly think of the male as "begetting," the Greek word
(*gennaō*) is also used of the female to indicate biological
ancestry. (See John 16:21.)

> "Monothelitism in the fifth century suggested that Jesus had
> only one will. This could be correct because it could show there
> is only one person in the incarnated deity. The flesh would not
> have it's own will, but the will of the incarnated Father" (142).

Here the *BWT* confesses to Monothelitism. This is an error,
because it denies the fullness and genuineness of Christ's human
existence. If He did not have a human will, He was not a human
being. Even if He were some kind of "heavenly man," He was an
incomplete "heavenly man," a kind of puppet or robot, a shell of
"heavenly humanity" lacking essential human components.

But, according to Scripture, Jesus did have a human will that
He submitted fully to the will of God: "For I have come down
from heaven, not to do My own will, but the will of Him who
sent Me" (John 6:38). The second phrase of this sentence, "not to
do My own will," indicates that Christ had a will distinct from—
but not independent of—the will of the Father. This is further
indicated in His prayer, "Father, if it is Your will, take this cup
away from Me; nevertheless not My will, but Yours, be done"
(Luke 22:42 [See also Matthew 26:39]). To deny the genuineness
of Christ's human will is Monotheletism. At best, Monotheletism
holds to an incomplete Incarnation, fragmenting human nature in
a way foreign to biblical thought.

> "Here is John's startling testimony about the Son of God: 'In the
> beginning was the Word, and the Word was with God, and the
> Word was God.' (KJV) 'In the beginning was the Word, and the
> Word was with God, and God was the Word.' ''Εν ἀρχῇ ἦν ὁ
> λόγος, καὶ ὁ λόγος ἦν πρὸς τὸν θεόν, καὶ θεὸς ἦν ὁ λόγος.'
> According to the Greek, the above rendering of the scripture has
> been translated incorrectly, for the sake of supporting the second
> God in the trinity. All translators change the literal order of the
> word **logos** to produce a separate person, God the Son" (143).

77

To translate *theos ēn ho logos* as "God was the Word" is an error. The reason all legitimate translations render this phrase "the Word was God" is not "to produce a separate person, God the Son," but because that is the correct translation. In a Greek phrase, the subject is identified by the article and by being in the nominative case. In this phrase, *ho logos* ("the word") is the subject. Greek is a synthetic language, with meaning determined not by word order, but by inflection. In this phrase, *theos* is anarthrous (without the article), and it is a predicate nominative. This means that it modifies the subject, attributing quality or essence to the subject. In this construction, deity is attributed to the Word.

---

"The Word who was made flesh and 'dwelt among us' proceeded from the Father without changing His essence so that the blood and the flesh of Jesus Christ would be of God's own nature" (145).

---

Again, the *BWT* denies the Incarnation. While using words like "blood" and "flesh," the *BWT* redefines them to mean something other than the blood and flesh shared by human beings. Thus, Jesus was not a human being. He has "God's own nature," so there is nothing of human nature in Him. This is denied by Hebrews 2:14-17: "Inasmuch then as the children have partaken of flesh and blood, He Himself likewise shared in the same that through death He might destroy him who had the power of death, that is, the devil ... for indeed He does not give aid to angels, but He does give aid to the seed of Abraham. Therefore, in all things He had to be made like His brethren, that He might be a merciful and faithful High Priest in things pertaining to God, to make propitiation for the sins of the people."

Jesus Christ "shared in the same" (*meteschen tōn autōn*) flesh and blood as all human beings. This introduces the purpose clause (*hina*). The reason He shared in the same flesh and blood is in order that "through death He might destroy him who had the power of death." The Messiah "had to be made like His brethren" "in all things" in order that (*hina*) "He might be a merciful and faithful High Priest."

It is the fact that Jesus shared in the same human existence as all human beings that qualified Him to defeat Satan on behalf of human beings and to represent human beings as their High Priest. A high priest must be one of those he represents.

> "The attributes and characteristics of all offspring are hereditary by nature. Therefore, 'Son of' always means born of the same nature" (147).

Although the *BWT* makes this claim, it denies it in its discussion of Jesus as the "Son of man."

> "No one can be saved by the flesh and blood of an Adamic person..." (147).

Here is the heart of the error: It is a denial of the atoning value of the death of Christ. The teaching of Scripture is that it is precisely because Jesus shared in human flesh and blood that He can redeem us:

> For both He who sanctifies and those who are being sanctified are all of one, for which reason He is not ashamed to call them brethren (Hebrews 2:11).

> Inasmuch then as the children have partaken of flesh and blood, He Himself likewise shared in the same, that through death He might destroy him who had the power of death, that is, the devil, and release those who through fear of death were all their lifetime subject to bondage (Hebrews 2:14-15).

Therefore, in all things He had to be made like His brethren, that He might be a merciful and faithful High Priest in things pertaining to God, to make propitiation for the sins of the people (Hebrews 2:17).

For He of whom these things are spoken belongs to another tribe, from which no man has officiated at the altar. For it is evident that our Lord arose from Judah, of which Moses spoke nothing concerning priesthood (Hebrews 7:13-14).

"As the holy Son of God, Jesus was raised from the dead with power once and for all. 'Concerning his Son Jesus Christ our Lord, which was ... declared to be the Son of God with power, according to the spirit of holiness, by the resurrection from the dead'(Romans 1:3-4)" (148).

At this point, the *BWT* omits a critical portion of the text: "made of the seed of David according to the flesh." These words testify in clear and certain terms to the biological connection between David and Jesus Christ: *tou genomenou ek spermatos David kata sarka.*

"As people supposed, Jesus is called the son of Joseph and the son of Adam. Neither of them are biologically His fathers. He is also called the son of Abraham and the son of David, but Jesus refuted all of this (Matthew 12:47-50; 13:54-58; 22:41-46.)" (148).

In none of these Scriptures does Jesus refute His physical descent from Adam, Abraham, or David. To deny that Jesus is the son of Abraham and the son of David is to deny what the inspired Scripture says:

80

The book of the generation of Jesus Christ, the son of David, the son of Abraham (Matthew 1:1).

Which was *the son* of Jacob, which was *the son* of Isaac, which was *the son* of Abraham, which was *the son* of Thara, which was *the son* of Nachor (Luke 3:34).

He shall be great, and shall be called the Son of the Highest: and the Lord God shall give unto him the throne of his father David (Luke 1:32).

Which was *the son* of Melea, which was *the son* of Menan, which was *the son* of Mattatha, which was *the son* of Nathan, which was *the son* of David (Luke 3:31).

And when he had removed him, he raised up unto them David to be their king; to whom also he gave testimony, and said, I have found David the *son* of Jesse, a man after mine own heart, which shall fulfil all my will (Acts 13:22).

Of this man's seed hath God according to *his* promise raised unto Israel a Saviour, Jesus (Acts 13:23).

Concerning his Son Jesus Christ our Lord, which was made of the seed of David according to the flesh (Romans 1:3).

who are Israelites ... of whom are the fathers and from whom, according to the flesh, Christ came, who is over all, the eternally blessed God. Amen (Romans 9:5).

These references do not include the many places where people referred to Jesus as the son of David. In these texts, the inspired writers of Scripture or Paul the Apostle declare Jesus to be either the son of Abraham or the son of David. To say that Jesus refuted all of this is to say that Jesus refuted the words of Scripture.

> "If the word 'seed of woman' is the biological seed of Adam ... we can dare say Jesus has a sinful nature. Since human flesh and blood is not an acceptable means of atonement for the sins of mankind, and because it cannot inherit the kingdom of God, Christ cannot possess earthly flesh at all (I Corinthians 15:50; Acts 20:28). We also cannot say His flesh was changed or glorified after resurrection. Christ's flesh is always the same in glory (Acts 1:11; John 21:4-15; Luke 24:29-31, 39-43). ... We must be sure that God the Father was not born of Mary (148-149).

The phrase "seed of woman" is definitely a reference to biological seed, unless there is clear contextual evidence that the phrase is used figuratively, as in Revelation 12:17. Even then, the metaphorical use is based on the literal meaning of the phrase.

The *BWT* overlooks Luke 1:37: "For with God nothing will be impossible." This statement by Gabriel to Mary, with specific reference to the conception of Jesus, means that it is possible with God for the Messiah to be biologically descended from Mary and yet not to have a sinful nature. If this is not possible, as the *BWT* asserts, Gabriel's statement is not true.

The *BWT* says that "human flesh and blood is not an acceptable means of atonement for the sins of mankind," when in fact they are the only acceptable atonement, as we have already noted.

The *BWT* denies the glorification of Jesus. None of the Scriptures given to prove this point do so. Instead, Scripture declares that the Holy Spirit was not given until Jesus was glorified. (See John 7:39; 12:16, 23; 13:32; Acts 3:13; Philippians 3:21.)

> "If we say Christ is from the biological seed of the woman, it would be true that we are believing Christ has a sinful Adamic nature, which in the sight of God is blasphemy" (149).

Thus, according to the *BWT*, to confess what the Scripture declares to be true is blasphemy! The *BWT* assumes that if Christ is from the biological seed of the woman, He has the sin nature. This is not true. The *BWT* asks, "If Christ has no human father, how can He be biologically earthly Adam"? (149). This is essentially the same question Mary asked Gabriel. Gabriel's response was to explain that the conception would occur by a miracle. The *BWT* overlooks God's ability to do whatever He wishes to do. It limits God's miracle working power by saying it would be impossible for a human being to be biologically descended from a woman without male sperm. But Gabriel said, "For with God nothing will be impossible" (Luke 1:37).

> "The Greek translation of I Corinthians 15:40-49 truly indicates that Christ is not made of the dirt" (150).

Nothing in this text indicates that Christ is not made of the same flesh as all human beings. Indeed, I Corinthians 15:39 points out, "All flesh is not the same flesh, but there is one kind of flesh of men, another flesh of animals, another of fish, and another of birds." If Jesus is a man, He has the same kind of flesh as other men. The idea of "heavenly flesh" appears nowhere in this or other Scriptures.

The "celestial bodies" and the "terrestrial bodies" referred to in I Corinthians 15:40 do not refer to "heavenly flesh" and "earthly flesh." The "terrestrial bodies" are those just referred to in verse 39 of men, animals, fish, and birds. The "celestial bodies" are those referred to in verse 41 of the sun, the moon, and the stars.

The "spiritual body" of verse 44 is not a body of "heavenly flesh" in comparison to the "natural body." The words "spiritual" and "natural" are adjectives modifying the word "body." In other words, the one is not a "body of nature" and the other a "body of spirit," or "spirit body." The context, beginning with verse 42 and continuing through verse 46, and including verses 51-54, indicates that the "natural" body is the pre-resurrection body; the "spiritual" body is the resurrection body.

The statement "the first man was of the earth, made of dust; the second Man is the Lord from heaven" (verse 47) does not mean that Jesus was not of the earth. This is a Hebraism, meaning, "The first man was only of the earth, made of dust; the second Man is also the Lord from heaven." This idea continues in verse 48, which should be understood as "as was the man [only] of dust, so also are those who are made [only] of dust; and as is the [One who is also] heavenly, so also are those who are [also] heavenly." In verse 49, the word "also" (*kai*) is actually supplied to make the point: "And as we have borne [only] the image of the earthy, we shall also bear the image of the heavenly." Verses 50-54 make it clear that the "spiritual body" required to inherit the kingdom of God is the resurrection body, a body that is "changed" from corruptible to incorruption, from mortal to immortality.

> "If we say Christ is the earthly human person in nature, then we are denying the oneness of God's person" (150).

The *BWT* equates belief in "heavenly flesh" with the oneness of God, claiming that those who disagree with its assertions are "denying the oneness of God's person." This is not true, but the statement does show the exclusivist nature of the "heavenly flesh" teaching. It is supposedly a requirement for a true understanding of God.

> "Neither John the Baptist, nor John the revelator, ever related Jesus to a human mother for they knew that woman within herself has no seed to beget child [sic]" (151).

An argument from silence is no argument. No case can be made from what someone did *not* say. But indeed, John the Baptist apparently did, by some kind of miracle, relate Jesus to His human mother. When Mary visited Elizabeth, "Elizabeth heard the greeting of Mary, [and] the babe leaped in her womb, and Elizabeth was filled with the Holy Spirit" (Luke 1:41). Somehow, the baby later known as John the Baptist recognized along with his mother Elizabeth that Mary was "the mother of [the] Lord" (Luke 1:43). The baby's movement was not unrelated to the visit of Mary. Elizabeth said, "For indeed, as soon as the voice of your greeting sounded in my ears, the babe in my womb leaped for joy" (Luke 1:44). In this context, Elizabeth, prompted by the Holy Spirit (Luke 1:41-42a) said, "Blessed are you among women, and blessed is the fruit of your womb!" (Luke 1:42b). To say that John the Baptist never "related Jesus to a human mother" assumes omniscience concerning every word John ever spoke during his lifetime and ignores his prenatal recognition of Mary as the mother of the Lord.

To say that John the Revelator never related Jesus to a human mother is also in error. The John who wrote Revelation also wrote the Gospel of John. John identifies Mary as "the mother of Jesus" in the following places: John 2:1, 3, 5, 12; 19:25, 26. These do not include the references where other people identified Mary as Jesus' mother.

John the Revelator also wrote three letters. In his first letter, he wrote, "Every spirit that confesses that Jesus Christ has come in the flesh is of God, and every spirit that does not confess that Jesus Christ has come in the flesh is not of God. And this is the spirit of the Antichrist..." (I John 4:2-3). There is no indication anywhere in the context that John means "heavenly flesh." By "flesh," John means "human existence." He also wrote, "This is He who came by water and blood—Jesus Christ; not only by water, but by water and blood" (I John 5:6). Although this verse may be interpreted in different ways, the context strongly suggests that this is a further reference to the Incarnation.

In his second letter, John wrote, "For many deceivers have gone out into the world who do not confess Jesus Christ as coming in the flesh. This is a deceiver and an antichrist" (II John 7). Again, there is no hint in the context that John means "heavenly flesh."

In Revelation 1:13, John identifies Jesus as "One like the Son of Man." This testifies to the genuineness of Christ's humanity. Since Joseph was not His father, the only way Jesus could be the Son of Man (humanity) is through His mother.

In Revelation 5:5, John identifies Jesus as "the Lion of the tribe of Judah, the Root of David." According to the "heavenly flesh" teaching, Jesus has no connection with the tribe of Judah or David. But John believed there was a biological connection, which could have come only through Mary, since Joseph was not Jesus' father. The word translated "root" (*hriza*) means "anything that grows like a root from one stem," indicating biological descent. It is used as a metaphor for offspring or progeny.

In Revelation 22:16, John records one of the most striking and powerful statements concerning the biological descent of Jesus from David: "I, Jesus, have sent My angel to testify to you these things in the churches. I am the Root and the Offspring of David, the Bright and Morning Star." The *BWT* says, "David could not be the biological father of Christ, for Christ is not from human seed" (page 131) and, "He also is called ... the son of David, but Jesus refuted all of this" (page 148). Jesus Himself says, "I am the Root and the Offspring of David."

As in Revelation 5:5, the word "root" in Revelation 22:16 is *hriza*, signifying the literal biological descent of Jesus from David. The word translated "Offspring" (*genos*) also refers to literal, biological descent.

When the evidence is considered, it is quite clear that to say that neither John the Baptist nor John the Revelator "ever related Jesus to a human mother" is quite wrong.

---

"He was not led by His own will for He has one will and Spirit (God the Father)" (154).

---

We have already seen the Monotheletism of the *BWT*, but now we see the claim that Jesus had no human spirit. This is similar to Apollinarianism, and we are left to wonder how the Spirit of God could "become strong": "And the Child grew and became strong in spirit, filled with wisdom, and the grace of God was upon Him" (Luke 2:40). To become strong in spirit indicates spiritual growth, a characteristic of the human spirit, but not of the Spirit of God.

We would also be at a loss to explain Luke 10:21: "In that hour Jesus rejoiced in spirit, and said, I thank thee, O Father, Lord of heaven and earth, that thou hast hid these things from the wise and prudent, and hast revealed them unto babes: even so, Father; for so it seemed good in thy sight." If the "spirit" in view here is the Spirit of God the Father, how does Jesus, out of a rejoicing spirit, pray, "O Father ...."?

If Jesus had no human spirit, how did He commend His spirit into the hands of the Father? "And when Jesus had cried with a loud voice, he said, Father, into thy hands I commend my spirit: and having said thus, he gave up the ghost" (Luke 23:46).

> "Earthly man's experience including temptations are a result of inherited sinful nature.... The experiences of the heavenly man Christ Jesus including His temptations are the result of the fulfillment of prophecies for reconciliation and propitiation for our sins (II Corinthians 5:19; Isaiah 5:4-5; Isaiah 53)" (157).

The *BWT* dismisses the reality of Christ's temptations, making them only "the fulfillment of prophecies." In this case, His temptations were not real; they were not a result of the genuineness of His human nature. They were, in short, part of a charade. The *BWT* assumes that temptations "are a result of inherited sinful nature." This is not true. Adam had no inherited sinful nature, yet he was tempted. Eve had no inherited sinful nature, yet she was tempted. Neither did Christ have an inherited sinful nature, yet He was tempted. Temptation arises from the freedom of choice that is inherent to being human.

87

Jesus was "in all points tempted as we are, yet without sin" (Hebrews 4:15b). If our temptations are genuine, so were His. (See also Hebrews 2:18.) Before He began His ministry, "Jesus was led up by the Spirit into the wilderness to be tempted by the devil" (Matthew 4:1).

> "The very name of Jesus Christ ... literally means Jehovah-Savior, Yeshua Messiah or Jehovah Tsidkenu, (Jeremiah 23:6; Matthew 1:21-23)" (159).

This is an error. Although the name Jesus (*Iēsous*) means "Jehovah-Savour," or "Jehovah will save," or "Jehovah is salvation," it does not mean "Jehovah Tsidkenu." Jesus is, of course, our righteousness, but that is not the meaning of *Iēsous*.

> "Jesus structurally was made in the likeness of men" (159).

The *BWT* teaches that Jesus had flesh and blood—although it was heavenly flesh and blood and not from Mary—but that He had no human will or spirit. Apparently, according to this view, Jesus was a kind of shell of a man with an external appearance of humanity, but devoid of the immaterial essence of human nature. Since all of human nature is fallen, and since Jesus could redeem only what He shared in, this means that Jesus would have been unable to provide complete redemption for the human race. As Gregory of Nazianzus said, "The unassumed is the unhealed." If there is any part of human existence in which Jesus did not share, that part is not yet redeemed.

> "The flesh and blood of Jesus Christ is equal with God the Father because it is the very nature of the Father Himself (Acts 20:28) (161).

Again the *BWT* denies any genuine humanity linking Jesus to the human race. He is not, in biblical terms, God manifest in genuine and authentic humanity. He is not God incarnate. It is not that God was manifest in the flesh, it is that the very flesh and blood is God. This is not what Acts 20:28 indicates. Acts 20:28 declares that the blood of Jesus belonged to God, because Jesus was God. The text does not suggest that the flesh was divine flesh and the blood divine blood.

"Since Christ was the Word of God made flesh, He cannot be the natural son of Abraham" (168).

Matthew wrote, "the book of the genealogy of Jesus Christ, the Son of David, the Son of Abraham" (Matthew 1:1; see also Luke 3:34; Galatians 3:16; Hebrews 2:16). "Genealogy" (*geneseōs*) indicates the biological descent of Jesus from David and Abraham.

"Christ did not come to partake of our earthly clay" (169).

Here again the *BWT* denies the Incarnation. The central feature of the Incarnation is that He "made Himself of no reputation, taking the form of a bondservant, and coming in the likeness of men" (Philippians 2:7). The word translated "likeness" (*homoiōmati)* indicates a genuine likeness, not merely an appearance.

"Therefore, a Christ with two different natures cannot be the true Son of God (John 1:1-14)" (170).

According to this statement, if Jesus truly was both God and man, He cannot truly be the Son of God. This statement contradicts Scripture, denying that Mary was the mother of Jesus in any biological sense.

> "Jesus designated himself as the 'Son of Man' numerous times in the gospels, while apparently none of His disciples or other Jews around Him ever spontaneously called Him by that title … the only reference outside the four Gospels is in Acts 7:56" (170).

The writer of Hebrews, quoting from Psalm 8, referred to Jesus as "the son of man" (Hebrews 2:6-9).

John wrote, "And in the midst of the seven lampstands One like the Son of Man" (Revelation 1:13a) and "Then I looked, and behold, a white cloud, and on the cloud sat One like the Son of Man" (Revelation 14:14a).

It is not accurate to say that the only reference to Jesus as the Son of Man outside the four gospels is Acts 7:56.

"It is a striking fact that God the Father, now manifested in His own flesh, (in the Son) was in the Old Testament called 'man,' Hebrew 'Iysh' and not 'enoshe' in its highest degree of perfection and spiritual essence. For it is written, 'The LORD is a man of war: the LORD (YAHWEH) is his name' (Exodus 15:3; or 'The LORD shall go forth as a mighty man, (Iysh) he shall stir up jealousy like a man of war: he shall cry, yea, roar; he shall prevail against His enemies' (Isaiah 42:13). Here again scripture calls Him 'Iysh'. Interestingly, this passage is found in the chapter where Isaiah gives a detailed account of the conquering Messiah. The point is that in these passages, the word 'man' is translated from the Hebrew word 'iysh or eesh.' As translated in 'Strong's Hebrew and the Greek Lexicon,' it means 'mighty, great man, male person', in opposition with the other Hebrew word for man, 'enoshe' meaning 'mortal, flesh, of lower degree'. Therefore, 'man' as 'iysh' qualifies God the Father showing His omnipotence and conquering power. God Himself has asked Israel to call Him 'Ishi', meaning 'my man' (Hosea 2:16; Job 25:4). When David said, 'But I am a worm, and no man (iysh); a reproach of men, and despised of the people' (Psalm 22:6), he was qualifying Himself as 'enoshe', a reproach of men, far from being a man" (171).

This section of *BWT* is filled with misunderstandings about the range of meaning of two Hebrew words translated "man," and it misidentifies the Hebrew words. The essential meaning of *'iysh* is "man, husband." The essential meaning of *'enosh* is "humanity, a human." *'Iysh* is not about the "highest degree of perfection and spiritual essence." It is about a male. Its inherent meaning is not about "mighty" or "great man," although in some contexts it may be used of mighty or great men. The idea of being mighty or great is not found, however, in *'iysh*, but in other words that modify it. For example, in Exodus 15:3 ("The LORD is a man of war"), the idea that He is warlike modifies *'iysh*.

Neither does *'enosh* mean "of lower degree" in opposition to *'iysh*. It does not mean "a reproach of men" or "far from being a man." It simply means "a human." This does not mean that *'iysh* is not human. *'Iysh* is a male human, a husband. *'Iysh* has

91

nothing to do with "showing ... omnipotence and conquering power."

When the LORD said to Israel, "And it shall be, in that day, that you will call Me *'iyshiy*," He did not mean they would call Him "my man"! The meaning is "my Husband," in contrast to "my Master."

The *BWT* quotes Isaiah 42:13: "The LORD shall go forth as a mighty man, (Iysh)." This is incorrect. The word translated "mighty man" is not *'iysh* but *gibbor*, a word that means "hero, warrior."

> "Some may misinterpret the title 'Son of Man' thinking that this title properly fits their Christ born of the virgin Mary, because, according to their view, He would have partaken of her Adamic nature; but of course this is totally in contradiction with the scriptural truth" (173).

Here the *BWT* overlooks the connection between the term "son of man" in the Old Testament and "Son of Man" in the New Testament. The Hebrew background of the Greek *ho huios tou anthrōpou* is *ben adam*, not *ben 'enosh*). *Ben 'enosh* appears only once, in Psalm 144:3. The Aramaic equivalent appears once in Daniel 7:13. In every other case where the phrase "son of man" appears in the Old Testament, it is *ben adam*. The essential meaning of *adam* is "earthling."

The phrase "Son of Man" does identify Jesus as a genuine human being, biologically connected to Mary. By denying this, the *BWT* sets itself at odds with the biblical use of the term.

> "We cannot say it is impossible for God to use the seedless womb of Mary to make the word flesh without partaking of her nature. Even today, scientifically, doctors have proved that surrogate mothers cannot contribute their own blood or flesh to the baby they carry in their rented womb. In the same way God has made it possible to send His only begotten Son" (174).

Here the *BWT* confesses to the belief that Mary was merely a surrogate mother. This means that the "humanity" of Jesus, such as it was—without a human will or spirit, was specially created by God and deposited in Mary's womb, or perhaps created within her womb but with no biological connection to Mary. This

92

means that Jesus is not one of us; He does not stand in solidarity with us; He has nothing in common with us.

> "Even though Christ was the son of the mighty God ... He appeared in the likeness of 'enowsh', 'anashh', or 'enash'; which means mortal, feeble, wicked, woeful man (Daniel 7:13 ...)" (175).

The word *'enosh* does not mean "feeble, wicked, woeful man." It means "human being."

> "The Son of man means Son of God" (178).

Here, the *BWT* completely dismisses the significance of "Son of Man." One is left to wonder why the term is used, since it means something else.

> "If the Word seed of Genesis 17 and Galatians 3:15-16 was the natural spermata, it would have been single spermata and Abraham must have had one son, Christ only. ... for Christ to be called the son of Abraham does not mean that Abraham is His natural father ... the seed of Abraham does not mean the biological seed. ... Christ was to Abraham a 'promised seed', not a biological seed" (179-181).

Paul means that Christ is the ultimate seed of the promise through whom the nations will be blessed; this thesis makes good sense of the promise motif in Israel's history. But he argues his case the way the rabbis often did: by attention to a grammatical peculiarity that was not actually peculiar. (As in English, the Hebrew term for 'seed' could convey either the singular or the plural [a collective], which Paul well knew—3:29. But rabbis argued in this manner, too; 'sons of Israel' meant either 'sons and daughters' or only the men, depending on what the rabbis needed it to mean in a given text. Paul's opponents no doubt read Scripture this way, and Paul responds in kind; he takes 'seed' as singular, a sense that the term can have in general but that does not seem to fit any of the Genesis texts to which he may refer [13:15-16; 17:8; 24:7], because he already knows, on other grounds, that Christ is the epitome of Abraham's line. ... Judaism nearly always took 'Abraham's seed' as Israel, which Paul would agree is usually what it means (Rom 9:7, 29; 11:1). But his argument in Galatians 3:6-9 permits him to apply this expression to Gentile Christians who are in Christ, hence in Abraham.[20]

Paul's emphasis in Galatians 3:16 reflects the larger issue of the use of the Old Testament in the New Testament, which is beyond the scope of the discussion at hand. In a given context, under the inspiration of the Holy Spirit, the writers of the New Testament may reveal meanings in Old Testament words and passages not readily apparent to those who have read only the Old Testament. But this does not mean they are denying the literal meaning of the Old Testament texts. Paul, for example, does not deny that the people of Israel are the promised seed: "Nor are they all children because they are the seed of Abraham; but, *'In Isaac your seed shall be called.'* That is, those who are the children of the flesh [Ishmael], these are not the children of God; but the children of the promise [Isaac] are counted as the seed" (Romans 9:7-8). In Genesis 21:12, quoted here by Paul, the word "seed" is singular, as it is in Romans 9:7-8.

"I say then, has God cast away His people? Certainly not! For I also am an Israelite, of the seed of Abraham, of the tribe of Benjamin" (Romans 11:1). Here, the word "seed" is singular.

In other words, it is not unusual for the word "seed" to be singular. (See, for example, Genesis 15:5, where it is singular even though the seed will be as numerous as the stars of heaven!) What is unusual is for Paul to make a theological point of the word being singular. When he does this, it is not a denial of the multitude of physical descendants of Abraham; it means that Christ is the ultimate physical descendant.

Matthew 1:1, Luke 3:34, and Hebrews 2:16 indicate that Jesus is the biological descendant of Abraham.

---

[20] Craig S. Keener, *The IVP Bible Background Commentary New Testament* (Downers Grove, IL: InterVarsity Press, 1993), 526-527.

> "John did not tell us that His flesh is earthy, but he does tell us that the Word was made flesh, and was not a ghost (John 1:14). If men do not believe like John … they are indeed of the devil" (180).

In the context of this statement and the larger context of the *BWT*, it seems that this means that if people believe that Jesus is biologically descended from any human being, they are "of the devil."

> "Jesus cannot have many fathers. … the mystery of the promised seed is hid from all readers of the Bible, and it needs revelation. … David is not the natural father or biological father of Christ. … David cannot be his natural father …. Since Christ was not born of man's seed, He cannot be the son of David biologically" (181-182).

We should note the very telling statement, "The mystery of the promised seed is hid from all readers of the Bible, and it needs revelation." This is an appeal to extra biblical revelation.

The Bible is clear that Jesus is descended biologically from David. The *BWT* says "'ginomai' is not used to refer to the natural offspring, or the biological seed." This is, however, precisely how the word is used in Galatians 4:4 and in Romans 1:3: "concerning His Son Jesus Christ our Lord, which was made of the seed of David according to the flesh."

This is a precise statement concerning the biological connection of Jesus with David. *Genomenou* is the genitive masculine singular form of the aorist middle deponent participle from *ginomai*. Jesus was made *ek spermatos*, "out of the seed" of David *kata sarka*, "according to the flesh"). That is, so far as the flesh of Jesus is concerned, it was made out of the seed of David. Mary was, of course, the seed, or a descendent, of David.

> Therefore, being a prophet, and knowing that God had sworn with an oath to him that of the fruit of his body, according to the flesh, He would raise up the Christ to sit on his throne, he, foreseeing this, spoke concerning the resurrection of the Christ, that His soul was not left in Hades, nor did His flesh see corruption (Acts 2:30-31).

95

In this reference to Psalm 132:11, Peter specifically declares the biological connection between David and Christ. Christ is *ek karpou tēs osphous autou to kata sarka* (out of the fruit of his loins, according to the flesh). To say that Christ is the fruit of David's loins means that He is literally and physically descended from David. This is further indicated in that His descent is "according to the flesh."

Paul agreed with Peter concerning Christ's physical descent from David: "concerning His Son Jesus Christ our Lord, who was born of the seed of David according to the flesh" (Romans 1:3). A literal and rough translation of this text would be as follows: "concerning the Son of him, the One being made out of the seed of David, according to the flesh."

In Revelation 5:5, John identifies Jesus as "the Lion of the tribe of Judah, the Root of David." According to the "heavenly flesh" teaching, Jesus has no connection with the tribe of Judah or David. But John believed there was a biological connection, which could have come only through Mary, since Joseph was not Jesus' father. The word translated "root" (*hriza*) means "anything that grows like a root from one stem," indicating biological descent. It is used as a metaphor for offspring or progeny.

In Revelation 22:16, John records one of the most striking and powerful statements concerning the biological descent of Jesus from David: "I, Jesus, have sent My angel to testify to you these things in the churches. I am the Root and the Offspring of David, the Bright and Morning Star." The *BWT* says, "David could not be the biological father of Christ, for Christ is not from human seed" (page 131) and, "He also is called ... the son of David, but Jesus refuted all of this" (page 148). Jesus Himself says, "I am the Root and the Offspring of David."

As in Revelation 5:5, the word "root" in Revelation 22:16 is *hriza*, signifying the literal biological descent of Jesus from David. The word translated "Offspring" (*genos*) also refers to literal, biological descent.

> "It is important to note that the Messiah's conversation with the Father did not arise because He was of an earthly human nature, but was God's work of intercession through the Incarnation for fallen mankind .... Was He suffering of natural hunger or thirst, because He was an earthly Adam with his own independent human spirit? No. ... Therefore through Christ's prayers, weaknesses, temptations, and agonies God was on duty ... Why was he hungry? Why was he poor? Why was he naked? Why was he thirsty? The answer is not because He was of an earthly weak nature, but He was a substitutional sacrifice on behalf of us all. ... People are neglecting the heavenly Christ by misinterpreting the work of God that was accomplished through the flesh and blood of Emmanuel" (187-188).

With these words, the *BWT* dismisses all of the experiences Jesus shared in common with us. His prayers, His suffering, His temptations, His agonies ... all are some kind of charade, a pretense with no substance. This is not at all the picture of His genuine human experiences as seen throughout the pages of Scripture. Concerning His prayers, the Bible records, "Who, in the days of His flesh, when He had offered up prayers and supplications, with vehement cries and tears to Him who was able to save Him from death, and was heard because of his godly fear, though He was a Son, yet He learned obedience by the things which He suffered" (Hebrews 5:7-8).

> "The man Christ Jesus ... has no human spirit but the father incarnate" (189).

We have already seen the Monotheletism of the *BWT*, but now we see the claim that Jesus had no human spirit. This is similar to Apollinarianism, and we are left to wonder how the Spirit of God could "become strong": "And the Child grew and became strong in spirit, filled with wisdom, and the grace of God was upon Him" (Luke 2:40). To become strong in spirit indicates spiritual growth, a characteristic of the human spirit, but not of the Spirit of God.

We would also be at a loss to explain Luke 10:21: "In that hour Jesus rejoiced in **spirit**, and said, I thank thee, O Father, Lord of heaven and earth, that thou hast hid these things from the wise and prudent, and hast revealed them unto babes: even so, Father; for so it seemed good in thy sight." If the "spirit" in view here is the Spirit of God the Father, how does Jesus, out of a rejoicing spirit, pray, "O Father ..."?

If Jesus had no human spirit, how did He commend His spirit into the hands of the Father? "And when Jesus had cried with a loud voice, he said, Father, into thy hands I commend my **spirit**: and having said thus, he gave up the ghost" (Luke 23:46).

## Conclusion

The "heavenly flesh" teaching misinterprets Scripture, appeals to extra biblical authority, and denies the genuineness of the Incarnation. It gives the false hope that there can be a biological change in the human body prior to the resurrection. It also denies everything the Bible says about the genuineness of Christ's humanity, destroys His solidarity with the human race, and renders His human activities – like His prayers – meaningless.